OH NO!
Maybe My Child Is Normal!

OH NO! MAYBE MY CHILD IS NORMAL!

Cliff Schimmels

Harold Shaw Publishers
Wheaton, Illinois

ISBN 0-87788-616-4

Library of Congress Cataloging-in-Publication Data

Schimmels, Cliff.
   Oh no, maybe my child is normal! / Cliff Schimmels.
     p.   cm.
   ISBN 0-87788-616-4
   1. Child development.   2. Child rearing.   I. Title.
HQ767.9.S37   1991
649'.1—dc20
                          90-43474
                          CIP

---

99 98 97 96 95 94 93 92 91

10 9 8 7 6 5 4 3 2 1

I t was a big day for the second-grade reading class. This was the last day for the student teacher who had been with them for the past ten weeks.

The children were excited but sad. Separation was something of a new experience for many of them. Finally, one little girl said with an air of expectancy, "But we will all see each other in heaven."

That prospect seemed to excite everyone, but there were questions.

"Will there be reading class in heaven?" someone wanted to know.

"Will there be tests?" asked another.

"No," answered the little girl who had the original idea. "There is only a test to get into heaven."

As I stood at the back of the room that morning and watched this story unfold, I was reminded of the awesome beauty of what Jesus taught us about children. He said, "Let the little children come to me and do not hinder them, for the kingdom of God belongs to such as these. I tell you the truth, anyone who will not receive the kingdom of God like a little child will never enter it."

I love children. I enjoy watching them at play; I enjoy their laughter; and I even enjoy wiping away their tears.

I enjoy teaching them, but Jesus tells me that that is not good enough. I must enjoy learning from them because in them is the mystery of the depths of being.

With all my training and experience, I can analyze, scrutinize, probe, poke, categorize, organize, and label. I can write reports, prescribe activities, and supervise growth patterns.

But in the midst of all this activity of what I can do, Jesus says, "Stay out of the way; let them come—don't push, don't shove, don't force, don't hinder."

This book is dedicated to all those adults—parents, teachers, and interested people—who take seriously the ministry of staying out of the way, and to all the children through the years who have taught me the ways of the kingdom.

Contents

1

NORMAL PARENTS, NORMAL KIDS

The other day my mother was thumbing through a recent edition of *Parents Magazine*, which she had picked up off our coffee table. Rather wistfully, she breathed a sigh and said, "I sure could have used something like this when I was raising my kids."

At first, I chuckled at this. *Isn't this cute typical talk for an almost-eighty lady,* I thought. *One who was born too soon, who worked against the odds, who would have appreciated any help she could pick up from anywhere?*

But all of a sudden I stopped chuckling. I remembered something important: *I know that woman's children.* In fact, I know one of them about as well as I know anybody.

I have studied her mom-techniques firsthand. In the language of the sociologist and ethnographic researcher, I have done a longitudinal study—53 years of it—and my conclusion is that *she doesn't need any help.* Her children are all perfect—intelligent, healthy, well-adjusted, and handsome. Well, at least *some* of them are *some* of those things.

But you get my point. Why did my mom need any magazine on childrearing? She had more theories than I had attitudes the way it was.

All this started my imaginative juices flowing. How different would it have been if my parents had had all the advantages of magazine help, books, and the ever-popular TV talk shows?

I Wonder . . .

- I wonder how they would have taught us to respect all beings of God's creation?

- I wonder if they would have still spanked us for riding the wild calves for sport?

- I wonder if they would have made us do chores before we did our homework?

- I wonder how they would have instilled in each of us a love for reading and learning?

- I wonder if my mom would have grabbed up my little sister the day she was hurt so badly and carried her in her arms almost a mile to get help?

- I wonder how they would have assured us of their love and care for us?

And I wonder how it would have all come out. If my mom had read those magazines, would I still have an addiction for cherry pie, Mark Twain, and crossword puzzles? Would our family still enjoy sitting around for hours, swapping the old stories with such fond memories and boring all the grandchildren to tears?

More imaginative juices! I wonder what my mother would have written had she been a contributor to that magazine?

That's not as far-flung a notion as it first sounds. After all, she was an expert.

Celebrating Normal

Almost every day I meet some mother with three or four young children in tow. After introducing me to each of her brood with vital details and vivid annotations, she gets that look of the far-off future in her eyes and proclaims, "When I get *this* bunch raised, I'm going to write a book."

Now *that's* a book I want to read—the book every mother would write about parenting if she didn't have her days filled with Little League and music schedules, and her hands filled with dirty diapers and broken toys.

> **Children are just people who can be raised graciously—if you don't have any.**
> **ANONYMOUS**

We have lots of the other kinds of books, books telling us about the strong-willed child, and the super kid in a tough world, and the hurried child. Those are all good books, and worthwhile. I certainly don't want to trivialize the mystery of childrearing. Nor do I want to undermine scientific research. This is not a plea for simplicity; it is simply a rally call for what's normal.

I would just like to celebrate *normal*—parents raising normal kids in normal circumstances. And doing it all in such an unusual way.

I do think I have something of a claim for this project. I could tell you that I have parents myself. But that would imply that we children are normal, and I would never want to make that implication in case some of you know my brothers and sisters.

I could tell you that I am a parent myself—a father of three who used to be children but aren't anymore. But that would imply that they are normal, and I wouldn't want to make that implication lest someone might know them.

But as a teacher and, more specifically, a teacher of teachers, I visit schools every day, and I get to see firsthand, up close, the interesting growth rituals of other parents' children.

Those are my models and goals—the thousands of normal children I see hanging around schools every day.

What This Book Is About

Let me warn you up-front about looking for something too profound in this book.

Don't spend much time searching for the "Things Are Rotten" section listing all of the ills of the universe. For one thing, I rather like this universe. At least it's the best universe I've ever lived in, and besides I do have this rather childlike conviction that there is a God in charge of things who has more power to make right than the human has to make wrong.

I also like children and adolescents. I enjoy their company, and I learn a lot from them.

Don't spend too much time searching for your yellow marking pen either. There isn't anything much worth underlining anyway. This is a book of affirmation and celebration. Since I have hoped to write the book you would write, if I tell you one thing that you didn't already know, then I fail.

So what purpose do I hope to achieve if there isn't anything profound here? Personally, I'm into little things. Everybody needs a book on the nightstand to use to read oneself to sleep at night, and I wouldn't be hurt a bit if you use this book for that.

> *Behold the child, by nature's kindly law, pleased with a rattle, tickled with a straw.*
> **ALEXANDER POPE**

I am also into chuckles and hugs. Maybe you could get in on both ends of these. Maybe reading this book will give you a chuckle, and maybe you'll find a spot that will make you want to chase your kid down and give him a hug—just for being normal.

But don't spend too much time searching for your kid to hug him. He'll come around when he gets hungry, and you can serve a couple of purposes with one effort.

Three Theses

Even if this book doesn't have anything profound in it, it does have a thesis—three of them in fact—about the same number as a good sermon, and that in itself ought to give the organization a little credibility.

#1 Every child is special.
In recent years, educators have really fouled up the language. It isn't any tougher rearing children than it

used to be, but you have to spend all that time just mastering the vocabulary.

We talk of self-contained and departmentalized classes—of gross motor skills and age-appropriate curriculum—of whole language and whole child instruction—of time on task—and attention deficits. It's enough to make you want to take a dictionary to the parent-teacher conference. But that wouldn't do much good because the teachers change the meaning of the words every couple of years.

One of the really unfortunate coinages is the term "special education" for "special" children. Of course, there are special children. Children with some type of physical impairment are special and need special education. Children with some type of inherent learning difficulty are special and need special education. Children who are born brilliant are special and need special education. Children who have an abundance of musical talent are special and need special education. Children who are just average are special, too, and need special education.

In other words, everybody is special, different, and unique, and has special needs and special demands.

Any parent who has more than one child instinctively knows the truth of this. With the first-born you make rules. With the second-born you revise the rules to fit the situation and personality. With the third-born you throw away the rules altogether. With those born after that the first-born makes the rules and gets angry at you because you won't enforce them.

> *In praising or loving a child we love and*
> *praise not that which is, but that which*
> *we hope for.*
>
> **GOETHE**

Maybe it's my bent to poetry, but I get excited about fingerprints. I look at fingerprints as a beautiful symbol of the Creator at work. If you want to check to see if your child is special, just look at the ends of his fingers. God superintended your child's construction even down to the tips of his fingers. And just as surely as that child has his very own fingerprints, he has a lot of his very own other things as well—personality, perspective, and problems. He is as special as his fingerprints.

To the parent, that little morsel of information has a definite application: There aren't any reliable cookbooks to make one perfect child. You can stir in a little of this and add a pinch of that and boil according to all the formulas you can find, and yet the recipe won't ever come out the same.

Hallelujah! Your child is special.

#2 In rearing children, normal is a broad range.

Sometimes people invite me to their gathering to give a speech, so I go and tell stories. More specifically, I tell stories about children and adolescents. If my story is good and if I deliver it well, I remind people of their favorite stories, so while I am telling my story, everybody else is telling himself his favorite story. Let me give you an example of how this works. Let me tell you one of my favorite stories.

A little girl was late getting home from school, and her mother was quite concerned. *(Okay, you should be into this by now. You should be remembering the time your own child was late, and you were so nervous that you paced the floor, gulped Maalox, and looked up the number of the police department.)*

When the little girl finally got home, safe and unharmed, the mother became quite angry. *(Are you still with me? Truth hurts, doesn't it?)*

Mother said angrily, "Where have you been?"

The little girl replied with the tones of a Mother Teresa, "My friend dropped her doll, and it broke."

"Oh, you stopped to help her fix it?" Mother snarled.

"No, you couldn't fix it," the little girl answered. "I stopped to help her cry."

I tell the story to make the point that there are some things in life—some emotions, some pain, some situations—that just can't be fixed. But helping a person cry is a big help, too.

That story is actually a good lesson for parents. Sometimes the only help we can offer is to help our children cry.

If I do a good job telling such stories, scores of parents will come up to me afterward to tell me their own special version of the story. That experience of identifying with someone else's story has happened to all of us. And since it has happened to all of us, I would have to call it normal.

For this book, we are not going to define *normal* as goody-goody and problem-free, but as a range that is big enough to include what most people are doing. The problem with this definition is that it's sometimes hard to tell what most people are doing. What most families talk about may not necessarily be what most families are doing! Yours may not be the only family on the block for whom the middle child's greatest achievement is to learn how to swallow air and burp at the dinner table. Just because that accomplishment rarely makes it into the annual Christmas newsletter doesn't necessarily mean that it doesn't fall into the range of normal.

#3 Panic is rarely the appropriate first response.

Although I don't enjoy it, I always learn from watching ace emergency crews at work—people like paramedics, firefighters, and police at the scene of an accident. They always work quickly but calmly. While everybody else around is losing his head, they bring order to the chaos.

That little art is probably the toughest lesson to learn in becoming an ace parent. Calm solves more problems than panic. Of course, there are times in parenting when hurry is in order. If your five-year-old is upstairs taking a bath, and water starts dripping through the dining-room ceiling, you may want to ascend the steps two at a time. But that's *hurry,* and it's different from *panic.*

Fathers, do not exasperate your children; instead, bring them up in the training and instruction of the Lord.
                                    Ephesians 6:4

Panic is losing your head and grounding your teenager for two years before you stop to consider who's going to stay home to enforce the punishment. *Panic* is punishing yourself more than the child.

Panic is overacting to a fad that is only going to last two weeks anyway.

Panic is labeling a child or allowing someone else to label your child before there is enough evidence to justify the label.

In short, *panic* is responding *abnormally* to *normal* situations.

Well, those are the three theses. They should provide enough structure for us to take a look at our own children—not dressed up like they are ready to pose for the family portrait, but in their everyday clothes with Kool-Aid stains around their mouths. Now that's normal.

And from there, we should have enough structure to take a look at the role our attitudes play in creating the kind of environment where being normal is not only okay, but encouraged—actually our goal. So let's talk about my house, and maybe even yours.

2

GREAT EXPECTATIONS

I f you want to raise a normal child, you have to expect *normal.* Let me restate that. *If you want to raise a normal child, you have to expect normal.* And *normal* is not to be confused with *perfect.*

Silly Notions

I don't know where we got all those silly notions about what to expect from our children. Maybe we spent too much time watching old family-life televison programs like "Leave it to Beaver," "The Donna Reed Show," "Ozzie and Harriett," and "The Patty Duke

Show." That's all dangerous stuff, surely designed to corrupt modern American morals. Those shows have done as much to give a distorted view of American family life as silly romance movies have given a distorted view of love.

You question my judgment? All right, let me ask you a question. When those kids went to their own rooms during the middle of the day, did you *ever,* even one time, see an unmade bed? Now that's pure fiction, but it's worse than fiction. *It's subversive.* It gives American parents the idea that this is the way it works in "normal" families, and then we all feel guilty, ashamed, and embarrassed when we live in a house where the only bed that is made on a regular basis is in the master bedroom.

If our kids were smart (instead of normal), they would forbid their parents from watching all the garbage on T.V. that gives such distorted notions. But I doubt that it's as severe as it seems. I suspect those kids on television only make their beds because somebody told them the cameras were coming.

Maybe we got our distorted views about expectations at family reunions by listening to the kinfolk talk. But again, kinfolk-talk is rarely about *normal.* It's about *perfect.* It's called *selective reporting.*

Maybe we got some wrong ideas about childhood and adolescence from our own memories. We remember our own growing-up days, thinking that's what normal is, and we expect our children to act like we did. But we weren't normal. We were perfect. (At least we were perfect in our memories of it. So that isn't much of a guide either.)

No! If we are going to work from realistic expectations of normal children, we are going to have to find our standards somewhere else. Maybe common sense would work.

> **It is NORMAL for a baby to be late. We can predict tornadoes, hurricanes, and the outcomes of political campaigns, but babies still come when they get ready.**

Exciting Moments

Let's be reasonable. As average parents of normal children, we can and should expect some exciting, memorable moments as we watch our children grow. These little moments not only provide the joys of parenthood, but they are significant in our children's health as well. Years ago a psychologist saw those moments as so important that he called them "developmental tasks." Let's look at them.

1. The first smile (or gas burp—the two look about the same).
2. The first tooth.
3. The first step. (But not necessarily in that order.)

4. The first word or something that remotely resembles a word.
5. The first sentence.
6. The first potty time solo.
7. Learning to count to ten.
8. Singing the ABC song and getting past "P" for the very first time.
9. The first round of patty cake (or whatever).
10. Dedication, confirmation, baptism, and other religious observances.
11. The first haircut (squirms and all).
12. The first bicycle solo ride. (Who among us will ever forget that great moment when Dad turned us loose, and we were on our own?)
13. The first day of school.
14. The first solo reading adventure.
15. The first night to stay at a friend's house!
16. The first real party.
17. Beginning music lessons.
18. The first date.
19. The drivers license (regardless of what that does to the insurance).
20. High-school graduation.
21. Marriage.
22. Becoming a parent and making us grand-parents (and notice how fast it all happened).

Isn't that a wonderful list, full of great memories of the past and memories to come? Makes you want to have a half-dozen kids just for the thrill of it all.

> *When a baby smiles for the first time, even the objective bystander knows joy.*
>
> *When my baby smiles for the first time, sunshine fills the day.*
>
> *When my grandbaby smiles for the first time, we stop the presses.*

Of course, the intensity of the joy of these events depends a great deal on how many times you have been through them before. Listening to your first-born sing the ABC song seems to have more intrinsic reward than listening to the fifth-born sing the very same song, even when she does it at an earlier age.

I remember when it came time for Paula, our eldest, to start to school. We prepared for weeks beforehand. We bought scissors, paints, a full box of 64 crayons, paste, glue, tissues, and a Miss Piggy lunchbox.

By the time Kris started to school eight years later, I remember saying something like, "The bus comes in twenty minutes. Do you have a pencil?" Somehow it doesn't take as long to prepare when you've been through it a few times already.

Normal Events

But there is another problem with that wonderful list. Those are the events, the developmental tasks, of *perfect* expectations. Sure, we can expect those wonderful moments, but we would be a bit naive to think that's all we can expect. Let's make another list of those events that parents of normal children can expect as well.

1. The first time the beginning walker falls down, cuts his lip on the dining-room chair, and has to have stitches. And we spend the next thirty years living with the false notion that it wouldn't have happened if we had been better parents.

2. The first time the fully potty-trained child has an accident. Have you ever noticed that these are timed to coincide with the sobriety of the situation at hand?

> **It is NORMAL for potty training to come with a certain number of setbacks.**

3. The first time your child lies to you. That has to be one of the most devastating moments in normal parenting. But I suspect it is almost universal. Every time I mention it to a group of parents, all of them look uncomfortable like their collars are too tight, or they are trying to suppress something.

    But the reason it's so devastating is that we don't know it's normal. It's not something you mention in polite conversation around the water fountain at work. You don't spend a whole month's long-distance budget calling all the relatives to announce, "Our child lied to us today."

But because it's so common, it meets our definition of normal.

4. The first time you are forced to realize that your child may not be the brightest scholar in class. There are several telltale signs by which we can get this impression. Maybe the teacher calls us in for a conference and spends an hour shaking his head and staring at us with that "really concerned" look on his face. Or every morning at 7:00 a.m. your child invents some new disease too serious to permit him to go to school. Or maybe the grades on his report card fall below sea level.

> It is NORMAL for teachers to look stern during normal parent teacher conferences. If you were walking through the woods and suddenly had to confront a bear face to face, how would you look?

5. The first time you try to call home with an important message, and your thirteen-year-old daughter has the phone tied up for two hours. That one doesn't need commentary, but it does happen, even in normal families, and *particularly* in normal families.

6. The first time you catch your child experimenting with immorality—swearing, drinking,

drugs, sex. I know that you have taught them well and have given them proper models. But for all your efforts, you haven't made them immune to the urges. Sometimes the urges will win out.

These are the developmental events within the range of normal.

Of course, this is only a partial list, but it is also an important one. These kinds of great events occur even in the best of homes. We may as well put them on our list of expectations because these joys of parenthood are just as real as those events of the other kind—the "perfect" kind.

The Power of Expectations

As we get our expectations in touch with what is normal, we need to keep another truth in the back of our minds close enough to a conscious thought to nag us. Our expectations of our children really do make a difference.

For one thing, we communicate our expectations. Let me restate that just to practice the art of restatement. We communicate our wildest dreams to our children.

"Oh!" I hear your first protest. "Surely, you accuse me wrongly! I don't dream wild and unrealistic dreams for my children. I never let my imagination run wild about what they could be if . . . I just want my children to be well-adjusted, typical, but happy people! That's all I ever hope for."

Yeah, sure. And the only reason politicians run for office is that they have this deep moral sense to serve mankind. Professional athletes love their sport so much that they would play even without those huge salaries.

We can be honest with each other. We're both normal parents. Admit it. There are those moments when we wonder what it would be like for our children to be rich and famous.

Now, I'm going to be honest with you and tell you a personal story. But I do it with a purpose. If I can be honest, so can you.

The night my son was born, I went home, went to bed, and didn't sleep a wink. I was so excited. Becoming a parent is such a special emotion—one that I won't cheapen by trying to describe it. And boy, I had that emotion. Besides that, I celebrated because our son seemed "normal." He had five fingers on each hand and five toes on each foot, and everything seemed to work. As you know, all that is a source of joy and happiness.

But that night, as I lay alone in the quiet of my own bedroom, I did something else. I prepared the speech I would be asked to give twenty-one years later when that "normal" son would win the Heisman Trophy for being the best college football player in the nation. In all modesty, I must admit that I put together a fairly good speech, there in my thoughts—and I was going to be so humble and so genuine. This would be a speech that would impress people and be one of my great achievements. I was ready for the occasion.

Don't tell me that we parents don't dream big for our children. How else do you explain that little flush of anger you see in the eyes of a dad at a Little League game when his son strikes out to end the game? How else do you explain that hint of frustration in a mom's voice when she looks at her teenager's report card and says, "Is this the best you can do in science?"

Oh yes, we all have dreams for our children. But our children have another name for those dreams. They call them *pressure*.

"Wait a minute." You now lodge your second protest. "I may have a dream or two for my child, but I keep those to myself. Those are my most innermost thoughts. There is no way that I communicate those to anyone, particularly to my child."

I wish that were true. I wish it were true for you, and I surely wish it were true for me. But I don't think it is. I sincerely believe that we do communicate those little dreams and thus pressure children in spite of everything we try to do.

> "What is it you want?" he asked. She said, "Grant that one of these two sons of mine may sit at your right and the other at your left in your kingdom."
>
> *Matthew 20:21*

Besides that, our own children are smarter than real people. They read between the lines. They particularly read "pressure" between the lines. Not long ago a college senior was telling me one of her childhood memories. She said that she had practiced the piano one evening. When she was finished and started up to her room, her father yelled from the den, "How long did you practice, dear?"

"About thirty minutes," she yelled back.

"Well, you won't get to Carnegie Hall on thirty minutes a day!" Father answered.

In normal situations I would have thought the story funny, and I might have even chuckled.

But there was a problem with this particular childhood memory. The daughter remembered it with tears in her eyes, and she concluded by saying, "That's the way parents put pressure on their children. Just like that. Every day!"

When I tried to convince the young woman that her father was surely just teasing that evening years ago, her friends, fellow college seniors, all chided me. "No, he wasn't. That's the way parents are. Always applying the pressure."

Do you think I ever communicated to my son my dreams for him to win the Heisman Trophy? Of course I did.

When he was in the eighth grade, he started organized football. Hiding behind trees and bushes, I sneaked in to watch one of the practices and at that point was struck with the awful truth that we would never achieve my dream. Fourteen years of polishing that speech for naught.

Did I tell him? Of course, I did. Not verbally and overtly—but I told him in little subtle ways. I told him because I was unhappy, and surely he knew that.

Incidentally, I think that is one reason why those junior-high years are often such killers for parent-child relationships. They come about the time we parents have to do some expectation readjustment, and that's painful.

"Yes, but . . ." Now you launch your third protest. "What's wrong with putting a few expectations on our children? What's wrong with a little pressure? I can't let my children goof off and waste their talent."

Of course, you can't. I agree with you. But those dreams, those expectations become wrong when they go beyond what the child has the God-given ability to fulfill. I have a thousand stories, and I'd like to share two of them with you now.

Not Interested in College

A mother came to me crying, actually heartbroken, because her daughter just didn't have any interest in going to college. The girl was obedient, respectful, cheerful, and could type more than 100 words a minute. But that was not enough for Mom. She wanted the daughter to go to college.

I don't want to discredit this lady too harshly because I am sure that she represents more parents than we will ever know. But I do want every one of us to catch a glimpse of the inherent tragedy. This mother had such a strong dream that she could not even celebrate the gifts God had given her daughter. She wanted another gift, one of her own choosing.

A Father's Dreams

A young man came to college knowing that he was to major in math. His first two years were miserable, and he was miserable, too. His grades were poor. He broke school rules. He lost interest in himself and others.

At the end of his sophomore year, the young man met with the college counselor—at the counselor's request. The student was about to be asked to leave school with a less than honorable discharge.

During this session, the student and the counselor both came to realize that the boy was majoring in math because that was what his father expected him to do. He actually hated math. He did enjoy literature, and would have liked to have been a literature major.

Now to make this a pleasant story, I should tell you that the young man changed majors, became a college success, and lived happily ever after.

But that's the fictional account. Real life is a little tougher. Do you know how hard it is in real life for a college student to look his father and chief financier in the face and say, "I am not going to major in what you have picked for me"?

This young man couldn't get up that much courage. He dropped out of school and was working as a clerk in a shoe store the last time I heard from him. He found this an easier choice than contradicting his father's dreams for him.

A Little Soul-Searching

Do I need to go on, or are those first two stories convincing enough? I am not trying to frighten you, but I would like for all of us parents to go through a little soul-searching.

Here are the questions, and we do have to answer them.

- Are my expectations of my children realistic?

- Do my children have the God-given talent to fulfill my expectations?

Now for the question that really hurts:

- Do I want what's best for my children, or am I expecting them to do what's best for me?

Since this is already deeper than I intended to get, I would hope that the pain of pondering serves as an appropriate summary for this chapter.

3
A PROPER PERSPECTIVE

The message of this chapter is quite simple: *Things grow*. In fact, things grow up, and quickly. I was going to start with an animal analogy, something clever and profound. I thought about asking, Do you know what happens to cute, lively, innocent little kittens? Well, they grow up to become cats. But there's a problem with that: my mother-in-law likes cats, and the analogy would probably get me into trouble.

I could have asked, Do you know what happens to cute, lively, innocent little calves? Well, they grow up to become cows. But the problem with that is that I like cows. Some of my best friends are cows, and I don't want to offend them with this story.

So without an analogy, I'll just ask the direct question: Do you know what happens to cute, lively, innocent little children? Well, they grow up to be teenagers. But have you ever thought of what happens to teenagers? Their fate is even worse. They grow up to become adults. And we spend most of our lives in that final stage.

You may be thinking, *That is such an obvious point, so why do we need to devote a whole chapter to it?* Of course, everybody knows that people grow and grow up, but I suspect that too often as our children are going through the various stages of getting there, we only know this obvious point in a philosophical and intellectual sense. I'm making a plea for us to get in touch with the reality of the principle in an *emotional* sense. Almost every minute of every day we need to tell ourselves, "Well, they won't be little long." When our child spills her milk in the restaurant and it gets all over everybody's feet, the table, and the floor, and the management looks none too happy about it all, we need to tell ourselves, "Well, they won't be little long."

A child is a most desirable pest.
                                    MAX GRALMICH

When the teacher calls to "invite" us for yet another conference in the endless parade of conferences and chats, we need to tell ourselves, "Well, they won't be little long."

When we tuck them in, listen to their prayers, tell a quick story, and kiss their little faces just before sleep takes over and makes them innocent again, we need to tell ourselves, "Well, they won't be little long."

Growing Up

Have you ever thought about how really short the growing period actually is? Let's look at some statistics of the obvious. The average person will spend only about $\frac{1}{40}$ of his life in diapers. For the mom of a little one, that's probably still a depressing piece of news. *Oh, no, I'm going to have to spend two years of my life doing this,* she thinks. But if we only spend $\frac{1}{40}$ of our lives in diapers, that means that we spend $\frac{39}{40}$ of our lives not in diapers. Isn't that refreshing to know?

The average person will spend only about $\frac{1}{25}$ of his life in junior-high school. That may be a statistic you need to hold on to. Write this on a big placard and keep it above your bed just for the promise: *Only $\frac{1}{25}$ in junior-high school and $\frac{24}{25}$ not in junior-high school.*

The average person spends only about $\frac{1}{4}$ of his life not married. Ponder that for a moment. If we are average, typical, normal, we will spend nearly three times as long married as we spend single. I don't know what it means—I just like the number.

> It is NORMAL for that early adolescent whose foot size matches his age to spill something at every meal, to stumble just walking across a clean carpet, and to bump his head on the door on the way to his own room. It is also normal for that same marvel to skateboard down the sidewalk at forty miles per hour while eating a snowcone, while reading *Sports Illustrated,* and listening to New Kids on the Block on his boombox.

Right Now and Later

In the midst of all this rapid growth, somebody has to keep a clear view of the obvious. Somebody has to maintain perspective. Somebody has to see the relationship, the correlation, the direct line between right now and later. If we don't, right now has a tendency to overpower with a sense of the emergency and urgency, and we lose sight of the idea that we have to go through right now to get to later.

Remembering that truth is the task of the parent who wants to raise a normal child. We parents need to remember it because no one else is in much of a position to do it for us.

Our children definitely can't see any relationship between right now and later. They have never lived in later. They have only lived in right now, and they don't understand later much at all. We can see this a thousand times a day.

> *Children have neither past nor future; they enjoy the present, which very few of us do.*
>
> **LA BRYERE**

We can tell them that they ought to save their money for later—until the family vacation to Disney World, until next week, or until college. We can tell them, but they just can't see into later as clearly as we who have lived through later already can see. They are really afraid that later might not come, so the urgency of right now has to be met some way.

We can tell them that they ought to take care of their friendships, make the most of their time, or make preparations for later. We can tell them, but it doesn't do much good. They just don't have any concept of later, regardless of how much their lack of vision frustrates us.

Their teachers also have trouble seeing the long-term later. I'm not accusing teachers of living in the same urge and emergency of the right now as children do, but they do tend to have a nine-month perspective. The average teacher will know my child for nine months of his life. In other words, that teacher has only about nine months to know what kind of person my child is, to see growth, and to achieve some sort of expectations.

Naturally, the teacher is in a bit of a hurry. When my child is not making rapid progress, the teacher understandably gets a little nervous. This is when the wise parent needs to say, "Well, they won't be little long."

Just to show how this works, let's do a simple exercise. Think back to the worst year you ever had during your own growing-up days. Of course you had a bad year. You had a year when the world was miserable, and as a result you were miserable, too. Identifying the year is not the problem, but remembering it is the tough part. Frequently, I find that many of us adults had such a terrible year at least once that we have conveniently blocked it out of our minds.

When I ask this question of parents in a meeting, the men in the group most often pick a year from the early teens as the miserable one—eighth or ninth grade. But the women will often pick a year earlier in the process—fifth or sixth grade. Again, I don't know what that means; it just seems interesting to me.

But now that we have identified the year that stands out in our minds, let's do the second phase of the activity. Call your teacher from that year and ask him or her to write you a recommendation. You wouldn't do that, would you? And that's my point. Aren't you glad that person's opinion of you is not the one you have to live your life with? Aren't you glad that the people in your life during that year didn't get so caught up in the right now that you never had a chance at later?

The Child is father of the Man.
                                        WORDSWORTH

This is why you as the parent must have perspective. You must see beyond today or the next two weeks or the next year. You must see a time, ten, fifteen or thirty years later when this little person will be an adult, and an adult for the rest of his life.

Timing

The first dimension of perspective is *timing*. The child experts all use their own calculators, and to demonstrate that they know how to use them, they work on growth schedules. They have all this down to an exact science. They have numbers and lists to tell us everything—the year, the month, the day, and the exact moment we can expect our child to perform every unique and individual accomplishment of his life.

By just consulting the charts, we can pinpoint the exact moment to expect the first step, the first word, the first sentence, the first day in school. Isn't it wonderful to be this precise? By knowing beforehand when all these things are going to happen, we can plan for them, invite the relatives, hire a band, and have a party.

I jest. We both know that nothing in life is that precise. And there's a reason for that. The numbers the child experts have are averages, and *average isn't normal.* Now, that may grab you as an unusual twist of a phrase, but I said it that way to get your attention. We need to keep this point at the front of all our thinking: *Average isn't normal.* Average is a *specific* number. Normal is a big wide range that includes average, but a lot of other numbers on both sides.

Too many times we read the numbers, panic, call Grandmother, and cry ourselves to sleep at night with the sad sob, "My child isn't normal," when all the time what we should be saying is, "My child isn't average." The two are very different matters.

In perspective, we must remember this: *In the span of eighty years, what's a couple of months?* So the child takes his first step at nine months or at twelve months. What's the big deal? The only principle at work here is bragging rights. You may have the oldest non-walker on the block, but that's more your problem than the child's.

Individual time schedules are not reflections on basic intelligence, wisdom, proper parenting techniques, or even genetic background. Time schedules are a gift from God, and should be celebrated.

Learning to deal with these numbers is one of the toughest prospects of parenthood. Regardless of how enlightened we may be or how much we try to avoid it, we still have to work out the task of balancing a child's uniqueness in personality and timing with the precise numbers.

For example, the government officials (that's another word for politicians) have decided at what precise time your child is mature enough to go to school. If your child doesn't happen to be on the state's schedule, you not only have to make a decision, you have to convince others that your decision is wise and in the best interest of your child.

> **It is NORMAL for a child to cry a bit the first day of school. It is particularly normal for moms to cry the first day of school.**

Patience is a virtue. That sounds so innocent and so simple that it is almost inaccurate in the understatement. In parenting, patience is the vital key that unlocks everything. It is more than a nice possibility. It is a mandate, an obligation that we owe to ourselves and our child. In our patience is found the magic of joy and happiness, both for ourselves and for the child. Patience sees through the bumps and scratches, through the tears and spats, and brings order to a world in disarray.

But as valuable as we know it is, as wonderful as we know it is, too often patience is hard to find. For most of us, patience is an act of will and not impulse. Patience is smothered beneath the urgency of right now that demands an immediate response.

But patience is the product of perspective. Patience is remembering that most of us will have about eighty years to work out the problem of this moment. When we come to understand this, then we will begin to comprehend something of the role of time in the work of being a parent.

Consequences

The second dimension of perspective is *consequences*. As we watch our children grow from babies in the cradle to fully functioning adults living in an adult world, somebody needs to ask on a regular basis, "What difference is this going to make in twenty years?" We need to see how this moment, which is happening right now, is going to be played out throughout the future.

> I have been reminded of your sincere faith, which first lived in your grand-mother Lois and in your mother Eunice and, I am persuaded, now lives in you also.
>
> *2 Timothy 1:5*

Personally, I am interested in this because I'm in the process of working on a new philosophy of life. I am working on the idea that if the crisis of the moment is something we will all laugh about twenty years from now, we may as well begin by laughing about it now.

When I was four years old, I spent most of my time under the leadership of my rather precocious cousin who was almost a full year older than I. One night, while our parents were downtown for some shopping, he and I slipped off to go into a variety store to inspect the toys, which were on display near the rear of the shop. While we were engrossed in our activity, the proprietor closed the shop and walked out the front door, locking it behind him. My cousin and I sensed, as bright as we were at that age, the full extent of our problem. We were locked in. Being the adventuresome sort, we went to the front of the store, pressed our noses against the big front window and stared at the people passing by until they stared back, laughing and pointing and ridiculing. Finally, someone went to get our parents, and another went to get the shop-keeper, who released us from our fate into the jaws of a worse fate—the arms of our parents.

Obviously, this little event has been the source of much joy at our family reunions through the years. Grown people have made complete fools out of them-selves, laughing uproariously, choking on fried chick-en, and spilling lemonade. Regardless of how many times I have heard this story told in all its vivid detail and description, it never fails to be the highlight of the occasion. But my question is a simple one: If this story is so hilarious, why didn't our parents laugh that night it happened? As I remember the event, it was rather sober and stern—no great joy and definitely no fits of uncontrollable laughter.

Why not? Why does a humorous moment only become humorous in the later? What prevents us from laughing during the original screening of the event?

> **It is NORMAL for a two-year-old not to be cute on command. Be forewarned. When you brag about your child, use words you won't mind eating, should the need arise later.**

The other day the mother of twin two-year-olds told me a story. Can you imagine being the mother of two two-year-olds? Do you want to hear what makes it even funnier? They are both boys. Now, in that situation, you have to have a sense of humor.

She said that she had just returned from a shopping trip to the market. She placed the bags on the dining-room table and went into another room just for a moment to assist her six-year-old. Frightened by the silence she heard pouring from the dining room, she rushed back in to check the twins. In her absence, they had discovered the bottle of liquid chocolate and were busy creating art, all around the room, dark brown lines on the table and the expensive tablecloth, brown lines across the carpet, and brown lines over all the chairs. She stood at the door in shock and dismay. One of the twins looked up from his captivating work and spotted his mom. With the excitement of a Michelangelo just putting the finishing touches on the ceiling, he exclaimed, "Look, Mom!"

She laughed. Now that's what I am talking about— the ability to laugh at the moment it is funny *as well as* in the future. That's perspective.

As parents, we need this perspective because, frequently, we need some idea of the later so we can test the worth of now.

Seeing Past Now to Later

A few months ago, a school invited me in for the purpose of observing and lending my opinion of two people.

The first person the officials wanted me to observe was a fourth-grade boy. This fellow was a bundle of energy, and in the classroom, that's a curse. He was all over the place. He could only sit still for a few minutes, then he had to get up. He moved around the room. He inspected the students' work. He wrote on the chalkboard. He looked out the window. He fed the gerbil. He would sit again, and a few minutes later, he would do it all over.

When my observation was over and I went to the door to leave, this fellow jumped from his seat, came running over, shook my hand, and genuinely thanked me for coming to his class to visit.

The officials and I met and discussed this person. Gravely, we shook our heads and considered our options. Should we get professional help? There is a legitimate disease that affects a few (let me emphasize that—*a few*) children called hyperactivity. But does this child qualify? Should we panic? What advice would we give to the teacher? to the parents? How could we deal with this problem?

> **Someone says "Boys will be boys," but he forgot to add "Boys will be men."**

The second person I was scheduled to observe was a fifth-grade teacher. This fellow was a bundle of energy, and in the classroom, that's a blessing. He was all over the place. He could only sit still for a few minutes, then he had to get up. He moved around the room. He inspected the students' work. He wrote on the chalkboard. He looked out the window. He fed the gerbil. He would sit again, and a few minutes later, he would do it all over.

When my observation was over and I started to leave, this fellow jumped from his seat, came running to the door, shook my hand, and genuinely thanked me for coming to his class to observe.

The officials and I met and discussed this person. They wanted me to write a letter recommending him as the county-wide teacher of the year. So I did, because I think he deserves that honor. But as I wrote, I couldn't help wondering what kind of a student he was when he was in the fourth grade. I wondered if the school officials had gathered for a somber conference about his energy level.

In this situation, the perspective required of a parent is tough work because it demands wisdom—the wisdom to see later. And that's difficult. But it is a common requirement.

For example, we ask, "When and how should a child be taught to read?" At first, that sounds like a question that concerns four-year-olds or six-year-olds or maybe even eight-year-olds. But actually when we ask the question, we need to be thinking of fourteen-year-olds and eighteen-year-olds and forty-year-olds because it's those people who concern us. As parents, we should be able to live with the fact that a six-year-old is not yet reading up to his potential, but the problem becomes acute when that six-year-old turns eighteen.

Isn't this fun? Aren't you glad your child has you for a parent instead of somebody who doesn't understand this as well as you do?

4

EXPERIENCE IS TO BE SHARED

Somehow during the period when the doctor first pats us on the backside and we sing our grandchildren to sleep, we accumulate a whole portfolio of experience. If we didn't, what would we have to talk about? How else would we be able to bore the grandchildren, the neighbors, and anyone else who is patient enough or diplomatic enough to listen?

But these experiences are more than subject matter for extensive rocking-chair conversations and illustrations in our speeches. These experiences that we pick up through life guide us, direct us, mold us, shape us, and actually play a vital role in forming us into who we become.

A philosopher once defined education as "the sum total of life's experiences." I don't know whether that's true or not on the personal level, but it does have enough of a philosophical tone to it to seem rather appealing. Through the process of creation, each of us is given inherent, unique qualities. But our experiences also help to educate us.

This isn't new information because we know the value of human experience. In fact, we know the value of our own personal and often minute experiences.

Have you ever gone to listen to a famous or important person give a speech? Have you ever noticed how often this person illustrated her points with accounts of personal experiences? And we go away saying to ourselves, "Well, I really know this person now better than I did before. I'm surely glad I went."

Have you ever seen those deep psychological films, the kind where they photograph in the shadows, and everything seems to happen in the dark? Have you ever noticed how often the plot of this whole two-hour endeavor hinges on bringing out into the open some hidden experience that is the key to understanding all the mystery of this person's life and everyone around him?

Okay, now that we understand the premise, let's translate it into normal parenting or parenting the normal child. The proposition seems simple enough: *If we want our children to be normal people, we help them accumulate normal experiences along the way.* In a nutshell, that's the issue.

> It is NORMAL for people who are not
> parents to watch normal parents, and
> make a list of those things they will never
> do when they become parents. It is also
> normal for those people to throw that list
> away about six weeks after the first child
> is born.

But accumulating normal experiences is not always a simple, normal activity. There are some barriers along the way.

#1 The Difference between Experience and Activity

In our modern society, most families have discovered the art of activity. We are busy people. We have dance practice on Mondays, Little League practice on Tuesdays, something at the church on Wednesdays, a birthday party on Thursdays, music lessons on Friday, haircuts at 4:00 p.m., supper at 6:00, etc. In ancient times before electricity and central heat, families used to hold informal meetings and chats sitting around a conveniently located stove somewhere. Nowadays, families hold those informal meetings in the station wagon enroute to another activity.

Have you ever noticed the nature of coincidence? In these days when food is rather plentiful and we need a bigger refrigerator to keep it in, the family activities have expanded so much that we need a bigger refrigerator door to put the schedule on.

We are always comparing our childrearing and family practices with the Japanese. Well, I've been in the Japanese homes, and I can't see where they have much family life at all. Their refrigerator door is much too small to put the schedule on.

Since we have filled our children's childhoods with activity, doesn't that mean we are also providing them with great childhood experiences? The kind that will give them stories to tell their own grandchildren?

Maybe, but maybe not. Activity is different from experience. For one thing, activity always comes in a mad rush, pounding us from every side, leaving us breathless in the wake. On the other hand, experience is like that special sea shell we picked up at the beach one time years ago. It may not be perfect; it may not even be particularly distinctive. But it is ours, our special one, and in the slow times of our lives we take it out and inspect it again, just as a reminder of what it was and why we have it.

For this reason, activity may even be a barrier to experience. We are in danger of rushing our children so much from one peak to the next that soon all peaks begin to look alike and the child doesn't even know when he is on a peak.

In fact, activity can be deceptive. It's often easier to give our child activity than to give him a relationship. No. That's not double talk. As our often-divorced television stars have taught us, it's sometimes easier to communicate with twenty million people than to communicate with one. And that's the danger of activity. When our children are involved in so much rush, it's easier to know a child through his participation in the activity than to know the child as a real person.

Let me see if I can illustrate that. A man I know was having a strained relationship with his nine-year-old son. For one thing, both of them are quite busy people. The father is busy doing the adult things of life—rushing to work, catching planes, and making big deals. The son, on the other hand, is busy doing the suburban kid things—sports, music, scouts, etc. When the two did have time to sit down together, they always ended up with crossed words and bruised emotions.

Well, it was time to take on another activity. They went to see a counselor. The counselor suggested that the solution to their problem would be to do an activity together. He recommended a baseball game. Now, doesn't that sound like a reasonable recommendation? Something fathers and sons *ought* to do together?

I was invited to go along. I'll go about anywhere to see a good baseball game, particularly if there is the prospect of a hot dog thrown in. But I would have been better off staying home that day. So would everybody in our party. Those two fussed and fought during the drive down, during the game, and during the drive home. They found absolutely nothing to be cheerful about or to agree on. I don't know what that activity did for the father/son relationship, but all that tension made me a nervous wreck.

About six months later, I mentioned the baseball game to the son one day as we were chatting, and he couldn't remember going. He had lost track of it in his mind. It had been just another activity in the midst of activities, and it hadn't been distinctive enough for him to register it.

On the other hand, one day I met a forty-year-old accountant. When I asked him how he had chosen to be an accountant, he told me a rather wonderful story. When he was nine years old, his uncle took him to a baseball game. As part of the experience, the uncle bought a score card. During the game, as the boy was carefully keeping track of things on that little card, the uncle casually said, "You do that well. Someday you will make a great accountant." And from that moment on, that fellow's life had direction.

> *Sweet childish days that were as long as twenty days are now.*
>
> **WORDSWORTH**

Do you see the difference between activity and experience? Now, which are you giving your child? In the midst of all the activity, are the two of you picking up any significant experiences, the kind that you will remember and that will have some positive effect on the future?

I coach college football. Of course, that's a source of experience as well as activity, but that's another story. Frequently, I have college athletes over to my house for food and friendly chatter. Many of these young men started the activity of football as early as third or fourth grade. They have been playing for a long time.

During our times together, the conversation will often turn to childhood experiences, and these are almost never about football. On the other hand, the conversation will often turn to football experiences, but these always begin sometime during the high-school days.

I find that interesting. People who care enough about the game of football to be playing it even as young men don't seem to have much memory of those early years in the sport. I wonder why that is?

#2 Observation

If you really want to learn something significant about being a parent, volunteer to help chaperone a class field trip. That's an experience every human ought to endure at least once in a lifetime. It's like a root canal. If you haven't done it, you don't know how to relate.

But there is quite an education in this activity. In fact, the education is so profound that I would advise prospective parents to volunteer as chaperones even before the baby is born. Of course, that could be risky. You may change your mind about even wanting to be a parent.

But children seem to come in three classes. Those three classes are never more clear than when they are on a field trip.

In Class One, we find the OBLIVIOUS. For these people, the end of the world is about three inches beyond the ends of their noses. They are totally wrapped up in themselves and their own creature comforts. There is nothing outside them worthy of their attention or interest. On the field trip, regardless of where you go and what exciting things you have to see, these people have three questions:

1) Where is the bathroom?
2) When's lunch?
3) Can we go home now?

At least there is one good thing about these people: they are easy to keep track of. If you miss one of them, no need to worry. He's probably back at the bus, lying across a seat with his earphones and radio turned up full volume.

In Class Two, we find the FUNCTIONAL. These are nice people. They walk in line. They keep up. They look around some. They have a nice time. But they don't attach any great importance to this particular day, and they don't see much purpose in any activity or life in general. They just endure—because that is what's expected of them.

Of all people, children are the most imaginative. They abandon themselves without reserve to every illusion.

MACAULAY

But in Class Three, we find the EXCITED. These people are on a field trip, and this is their chance of a lifetime. They have never seen such interesting things. They are so involved that they can't keep up. You are always stopping the convoy to look for one of them. They don't mean to be rude, but they have a hard time staying within the boundaries. If you don't constantly watch them, they will jump over those little velvet ropes that are used to control the crowd. They always want to inspect a little closer.

Finally, you decide you have had enough of this, so you pick out the most excited of the excited and make him hold your hand during the guided tour. But that's a mistake, too. Not only does this child tug and pull until you think your arm is going to come out of the socket, but he also provides you with a running commentary so filled with enthusiasm that you don't have time to listen to the whines of the OBLIVIOUS.

When it comes time to go home, the excited child pouts a bit, and is always the last one on the bus. But on the way home, this child will jump up at least once, run to the front of the vehicle (despite the driver's protest), thank you for taking them to such a neato place, and ask when you can all go back.

When I was a boy, my father used to say to me, "You've got to learn how to have a good time." I thought that was about the dumbest thing I had ever heard. How can you learn to have a good time? I always thought that good times are extrinsic events, outside us, a product of the circumstances. At least that is what I thought until I started chaperoning field trips. Now I know what my father had in mind. You do have to learn how to have a good time. That's what we learn from the EXCITED.

> **It is NORMAL for some children to enjoy hammering more than they enjoy reading.**

Obviously, I like the EXCITED. I wish all children could be like that, could suckle deep from this moment, living it to its fullest, letting it make an impact, letting it change them.

Since I value this so much, my next logical task would be to list five steps you could go through to help your child acquire the art of observation so that he could make the most of his experiences. That's what I could do, but it wouldn't do much good. The truth is that I don't know how to teach that to a child. I don't know the steps you go through, so I would just be making it all up. What I suggest may or may not work.

So instead of making a list of logical teaching steps, I am going to suggest that you use the Think System. I discovered the Think System of learning from watching reruns of the old movie, *The Music Man*. This was Professor Harold Hill's answer to music lessons: If you think "The Minuet in G," you should be able to play it. And the same is true for you: If you think you want to teach your child the fine art of observation, if you think you want your child to go through life as one of the EXCITED, you probably *are* teaching him that.

#3 Sharing

There's an old joke about a minister who sneaked off one Sunday afternoon to play a round of golf. In his infinite wisdom, God punished the minister by enabling him to make two holes in one. The punishment was that the minister wouldn't be able to share it with anyone.

That's why experience is so rich for us. It brings us joy when it happens and it brings us joy when we tell it to someone else.

In helping our children accumulate enough childhood experiences to last them a lifetime, we have to remember this part about the need to share. We have to listen to them. And not only listen, but listen intently.

These commandments that I give you today are to be upon your hearts. Impress them on your children. Talk about them when you sit at home and when you walk along the road, when you lie down and when you get up.

Deuteronomy 6:6-7

At this point, I hope you don't expect me to go off into a long discussion of the proper methods and techniques of listening to your child. Wiser people than I have done this already, and if you need to know, you can buy their books. I can't even give you much of a review of those books—which ones are good and which aren't—because, frankly, I haven't read them.

Maybe I don't know as much about listening to children as I should know, but I do know that we need to do it. I do know that children are real people; and like real people, some are boring, some are rather tedious in their sharing, and some really know how to spin a yarn. But regardless of their storytelling gift, you still need to listen.

I also know that listening to children is like listening to any other real person. If you pay attention, you can really learn a lot. Now, that seems to me to be the secret to the method, and that's why I'm afraid to get into a discussion of the "proper" techniques. Such a discussion might give the impression that listening to your child is some kind of a duty to be performed according to specific rules.

I would rather suggest that we look at listening to our children as an opportunity to become a little better informed and a little wiser.

The proper way to listen to your child is an *attitude* rather than a *method*. But it is an attitude that pays dividends. Where else but listening to my own children would I have learned such rich truths about the universe as these?

- Lemmings are rats who live in Scandinavia, and when they get too many, they all go jump in the lake.

- George Washington kept a mattress, and that's how he died.

- Symbols are dumb. Writers ought to say what they think.

- Blue is prettier than red because you can look at it while you're sitting still.

- Detentions are never fair.

- Books should not be long, because if they are too long, people figure them out way before they get to the end of the story.

These are just some examples of the shared experiences of growing up, and that sharing makes life richer for both of us. (Actually, I just threw those in to impress you with a few cute things my children said to me. I enjoy telling them, but it is hard to work them into a normal conversation.)

Now that I have said all that, you're probably nodding your head, saying, "Yes, I'm convinced." But let me remind you that this mutual sharing is valuable *regardless* of the age of our children. I suspect that some of us do this better when they are at one particular age than when they are at another. Let me illustrate this with a rather crucial point.

Reading experts tell us the value of parents reading to children, and wise parents have heeded the advice. When our children are quite young, we read to them. As they learn to read themselves, we listen to them read. We actually get involved in the process. We act surprised. We ask questions. We get discussions started. And reading becomes a shared experience. Quite frequently, when I hear adults speak of childhood experiences and memories, they mention the shared experience of reading together. It is a wonderful time, and in the process a wonderful thing happens—the bonding of parent and child.

> **It is NORMAL for adolescents to think their parents are totally and completely incompetent so they say such things as, "That is soooo dumb."**

But as our children get older and more proficient in their ability to read, we expect them to be just as avid readers, but we don't share with them anymore. Do you see the dilemma here? When our children are young, reading is one of the sources of our time together. As they get older, our choices in reading materials actually serve as something of a wedge between us.

Occasionally I will ask the parents of a teenager, "What is the last book your child read?" Most of the time the parent can't answer. That tells me there has been no sharing. I wonder if that is one of the reasons why our young people lose interest in reading as they move through the upper stages of elementary school. It ceases to be a shared activity.

In recent years, I have noticed some junior-high and even high-school teachers spending a few minutes each day reading to their students. The critics are having a field day with this. "The purpose of schools is for the student to learn to read for himself," they tell me. And that may be true. But the purpose of reading is the experience, and experience needs to be shared.

5

ALL
IN ORDER

Frequently I visit in my daughter's home. Across the street is a Tot-Lot—a children's playground. In reality, it's a small, simple thing with an old swing set and a sandbox.

But this little playground is the popular meeting place of about a dozen neighborhood kids—from ages two-and-a-half to ten. And they spend hours there every day. Although they do come and go, they swing on the swings, slide down the slide, teeter-totter, and make farms and castles in the sandbox. They are children at play.

Being too old myself to play anymore, watching children at play has become one of my favorite activities. That's one of the differences between parents and grandparents. As parents, we tend not to enjoy watching play so much because we still have that urge to participate—not only to be active, but to be active in their lives.

As a grandparent, I have long ago been able to defeat that urge to be too participatory. I now enjoy watching, and I do it well. I suffer no guilt at all.

Children are a beam of sunlight from the Infinite and Eternal with possibilities of virtue and vice—but as yet unstained.
LYMEN ABBOTT

But I have learned something watching those children at play. Well, I didn't actually learn anything new, but I did reaffirm an amazing old observation: even with the freest kind of activity with no adult anywhere in sight (except for a doting old grandpa across the street) those children nevertheless play by the rules.

They have rules for their activities. Swingers get only a certain amount of swings before they have to share. Sliders must take turns, and it's no fair taking cuts. Sandbox architects are allowed only so much time in the box.

I don't know where the rules came from. Maybe there was a legislative forum. Maybe there is a young dictator in the crowd. But they have rules.

> **It is NORMAL for children to think their parents are infallible so they say such things as, "My daddy is stronger than your daddy."**

Of course, legislation alone doesn't control the masses. There always has to be an executive branch to enforce the rules, and this little Tot-Lot empire is no exception. There are rule violators who must be punished. As best as I can observe, that punishment usually consists of being yelled at and called names.

Frequently, the violator, at being subjected to all this verbal abuse, will respond with a self-imposed exile. He'll ride off on his bike, circle the block a couple of times, rejoin the group, and begin to play by the rules again.

Now, how do you explain that—these children playing by rules? We could make light of the whole thing and say that they are only copying adults. Maybe so, but they still choose this aspect of adult life to copy.

No! I would rather say it more strongly. I believe I'm willing to say, rather matter-of-factly, that children have a natural proclivity for rules.

But that's too specific. I want to make this even broader and stronger. I believe that children have an inherent need and longing for order.

Now that's a proposition that merits a little attention. Let's phrase it as a mandate. *One of my principal roles as a parent is to provide my child with the circumstances for an ordered life.*

Before you get all disturbed and start accusing me of being an ogre and a tyrant who goes around stealing spontaneity and creativity from little children, let's take a look at some of the specific arenas of this ordered life.

The Arena of the Familiar

Not long ago, my three-year-old granddaughter and I spent four days in a row taking a four-hour automobile trip each day. At the beginning of the excursion, she handed me her tape and asked if I would play it in the machine as we traveled.

Since she said "please" with such conviction, I consented. We played her tape—a cute little thing of children singing the old familiar Sunday-school tunes with an invitation to sing along.

When we had played the tape all the way through, we played it again. And again. And again. We played her tape all day every day. We played only her tape.

When she dozed off, I would sneak in my tape, but she would quickly regain consciousness. She'd say, "Please?" with conviction, and we would resume playing her tape.

How do you explain sixteen hours of listening to the same tape over and over? Simple. It's her penchant for order. She doesn't like surprises—not in her music—not in her world.

If you are the kind of parent who does what you ought to do with your child, and surely you are or you wouldn't be reading this book, you have already seen this in your night-time reading and storytelling. Your child always wants to hear the same story over and over until you have the thing so memorized that you catch yourself reciting it when you gather up the groceries at the supermarket.

All of us have had the experience firsthand, and the experts have even explained it for us—often in terms I don't understand. But I still say that all this demand for the familiar indicates that it is normal for children to want order.

Of course, we have been talking about young children. At what age does a person grow out of this innate need for order? Maybe at about eighty-six, I would guess. I don't want to make the case that we are all locked into tradition so deeply that we can't experiment and launch out into the unknown; but as parents involved in the process of trying to figure out what makes our children tick as they do, it's important to remember that it's normal to have this need.

Our son went through the 180 days of his eighth-grade school year wearing the same blue jeans and the same polo shirt. We are poor, but we're not that poor. We surely could have afforded a second costume even if it was like the first. In fact, we bought him one—several as I remember, but he still wore the same stuff.

At that age, he didn't want any surprises. He got the look right, and there wasn't any need to change. In that junior-high world of abrupt, frequent, and continuous change, he was looking for something constant, something dependable, something that would give his life a little order. Maybe just dressing the same way every day didn't seem like such a big achievement to us, but it was to him.

> **It is NORMAL for parents to suffer pangs of guilt.**

As the old world adage tells us, "We get too old soon and too late smart." But I wish I had been smart enough to have understood what I just explained when my son was in the eighth grade.

My tongue wouldn't have been so sore that whole year. Every morning when he came in ready for school in those same jeans and shirt, I managed not to say much, but I did have to bite my tongue a lot. I still have the scars—scars that remind me of how dumb we can be as parents and how often we make life worse for ourselves than it needs to be. After all, raising normal children is usually rather pleasant, once we understand what normal is.

Of course, some lessons we keep learning throughout our lives.

Not long ago, I spent three days with three other men in rather close quarters. In that situation, we four shared a bathroom. But that wasn't a problem. Four men can share a bathroom, providing no one sings in the shower or has to be alone to write poetry or something.

But this was one of those configurations where the shower was inside the bathroom and the preparation sink was on the outside. That's where the problem came. Every red-blooded adult male knows that the proper sequence is to shave before you shower. That is so logical and so obvious that it should be universal knowledge. But not a single one of those other three guys understood that simple principle. Everybody else showered before he shaved. That's almost a moral corruption. For the sake of peace and convenience, I did it backwards, too, but I didn't like it. It ruined my whole day.

Now I understand why we played Alyssa's tape for sixteen hours.

The Arena of Love

Not long ago a college senior stood in my office late one night. He was the epitome of the burned-out student. A usually neat person, he was disheveled. He had bags under his eyes and stacks of books under his arms. Throughout our conversation, he fidgeted the fidget that told me he was torn between his desire to stay and talk and his need to get back to his room to study.

As he stood to leave, I sensed that I needed to say something; so I asked simply, "Why are you driving yourself this way?"

He turned and looked at me with sad eyes and said, "I want my father to love me."

Let's summarize this—or as your ninth-grade English teacher said, "Let's make a précis."

This need to feel loved is one of the most powerful forces in all the world. When it is fulfilled, it brings joy and happiness beyond expression. When it isn't fulfilled, that vacuum can be devastating to even the strongest person.

In our effort to rear normal children, the very first task is to make sure that the child is assured of our love. I am not even going to ask you if you love your child. That's too easy. Instead, I am going to ask the tough question: Does your child *know* that you love him?

In this age of instability and change, our children must grow up in a world filled with frequent examples of unstable and vacillating love. But we know that already. We see it everywhere around us—on television, in the movies, at school, at home, even in the grocery store. There is no need to dig up that information or those stories here. We all know the kind of "love" we're talking about.

So we can forego the problem and concentrate on finding a conclusion. If our children are going to experience the order in their lives that comes from being able to depend on a constant, unwavering love, we have to find the method of communicating that love now and all throughout their lives.

> Love is patient, love is kind. . . . It always protects, always trusts, always hopes, always perseveres. Love never fails.
>
> *1 Corinthians 13:4, 7-8*

Wow! That's a scary order. I suspect that as parents we often feel we fail in this. In fact, our own children may accuse us of failing. During those moments when they suspect that they may not get their way and they grab for their most persuasive weaponry, they may drop little hints designed to make us feel guilty.

Children do have a habit of saying such things as:

"You don't trust me."
"Everybody else will be there."
"I didn't ask to be born, you know."
"You let my older brother go. You must love him
     more than me."
"I have to do the dishes every night."
"What difference does it make that the grade is low?"

Normal children do occasionally challenge their parents' love with such statements.

> **It is NORMAL for adolescents to have
> vocabularies that include: "Soooo," "You
> don't trust me," "I'm so humilified,"
> "Nobody likes me," "I want to move away
> from home."**

Now that I brought it up, you probably expect me
to give you some list of brilliant comebacks to squelch
that line of reasoning and still perpetuate the assurance of our love. But I don't know any brilliant
comebacks; and if I did, they probably wouldn't work
with your child anyway.

Usually, at those times when I stood at the receiving
end of such cutting remarks, I had the composure and
wit to answer with retorts like, "Oh, yeah?" But since
I am older and wiser now and since we are talking
about your child instead of mine, I might offer a couple
of suggestions.

---

*Children in a family are like flowers in a
bouquet: There's always one determined to
face in an opposite direction from the way
the arranger desires.*

MARCELENE COX

Just for once, you might try agreeing with the child.
Wouldn't that be fun, just once? As your young lawyer

is presenting his best plea, agree. "Yes, dear, you're absolutely right. I have been a total fool about this. Here's a thousand dollars. Go buy your motorcycle."

That ought to take him by surprise. This approach will help you check to see if he is committed to the cause or is just arguing for the sake of the argument. But before you try that, make sure you know your child well. One of you could have cardiac arrest from something this shocking.

Incidentally, I am only partly jesting here. I do think that sometimes our children make unreasonable requests and start arguments just to be reassured that we really do love them.

My second suggestion is based on that same thought. Right in the middle of the protest, just grab your child and hold him close to you in a big, loving hug.

I actually learned this from my son. When he was a little fellow, I would hold him on my knee to scold him about some misdemeanor. In the middle of my presentation of ethics, morality, and right and wrong, he would reach up and kiss me. It worked for him. Why not try it ourselves?

Although I am not going to provide you with some check list to follow to demonstrate love, I do want to give you a challenge. In order to assure your child of your love, you must know yourself that you love him, and that you will *always* love him *regardless of what happens*. You must never doubt that.

The Arena of Environment

Have you ever noticed how even a great cook is disoriented in someone else's kitchen? We all have our own individual organizational scheme, and we order the segments of our environment according to that scheme.

Oh, maybe at the beginning we sort of stumble onto some of those organizational schemes by happenstance. But after a while, when habit sets in, the way we organize things becomes an inseparable part of us, almost as significant as our fingerprints.

Children desire an orderly environment, too. The only problem is that they may not know it. Sometimes when you look in a child's room and most of the time when you look into a teenager's room, you might have a hard time believing that this is a person who has an inherent need for order.

But I still think so. I've become convinced of this while visiting first-class preschool and high-school English classes. I've noticed a pattern all the way through. The more organized the environment, the calmer the class and the greater appreciation the students have for the teacher.

I've seen order work almost as a miracle drug. For example, last fall, I visited a seventh-grade class where the teacher was having some rather serious classroom management problems. Neither threats nor tears seemed to do much good. Finally almost in desperation, she cleaned the classroom, threw away some extraneous material, did some cataloging, and brought some order to the physical environment.

That did wonders. The students calmed down, and this became a rather normal, slightly active class.

Now that observation ought to say something to us as parents. Although they may not give us any clues, probably our children are striving for an ordered environment. Maybe we could spend some valuable time helping them devise a system of putting their toys away and folding their own socks. That may be the key to helping your child get control of his whole life.

Because I have to spend my life around other people's children, I have become concerned about this need for order during the era of the broken home. I'm concerned about those children who basically are asked to live in two homes, two different environments, two different organizational standards. I hope the adults in their lives understand their need for order.

The Arena of Family Roles

In your normal American family of 2.4 children, you have your first-born, you have your second-born, and then you have that point-four person.

A noted psychologist who lives out somewhere where the sun is hot has written a book explaining what it means to be the first-born, the second-born, and the point-four-born. It's fun reading, and it makes a valuable point. Regardless of where it comes from, there is, nevertheless, some order attached to those family roles.

There are rites, privileges, and responsibilities for the first-born; rites, privileges, and responsibilities for the second-born; and rites, privileges, and responsibilities for the point-four-born.

There may be some who want to protest this. But that's the way the system works.

The first-born gets to pick which room he wants; the second-born of the same sex has to wear hand-me-downs. The baby sits closest to mother at the dinner table, but is compensated for that by getting to eat the drumstick.

The first-born gets the excitement of being the first one to survive a developmental task: tying his shoes, riding a bike, starting school, sleeping over, driving a car, going on a date. But the subsequent-born, although they can't be the first to do those things, compensate by getting to do them at an earlier age.

But the first-born still has the final word. She gets to complain about the injustice of it all and to offer counsel on how the parents ought to be rearing the young ones. But this, too, is normal and necessary.

The Arena of Rules

This brings us back to our opening point. Children want rules. They seek rules to achieve some kind of order in their existence. If they can't find rules from somewhere else, they make them up themselves.

We parents can help in cutting down that hunt-and-seek time by just giving them some rules. Normal families have rules. We have rules about bedtime, homework, Sunday-school attendance, television watching, chores, table conduct, and dating.

> *Your child is the one who tells in the street what his parents say at home.*
> **ANONYMOUS**

Of course, as the family grows, you may find that in spite of how comprehensive you may think you have been in making your rules, there is always a need for even more rules. There are emergency rules and ad hoc rules. For example, you may need a rule about filling the dog's water dish out of the toilet bowl. (As you can tell, some of the contingencies of normal families are not always covered in the child-expert publications.) You may need a rule about touching or tickling or teasing. You may need a rule about tooth-paste squeezing or soap use. Or you may even need a rule about whose rule is to be obeyed first.

Of course, as you establish these rules, you need to keep two points in mind. First, *just as children want rules, they want to know the consequences of breaking the rules.* To learn that, they often resort to logical action. They break the rules.

Too often, we parents get confused at this point. We tend to think that because they break the rules, they don't want the rules, but that isn't necessarily true. They're just trying to establish the boundaries. Without boundaries, there isn't much order—or freedom.

But that leads to our second point: *You may not want rules to cover every contingency.* In other words, when you know that a rule may cause a protest, pick your battling points judiciously. Make sure the issue is worth fighting about. If it isn't, let it go. There will be plenty of others to fill its place!

6

GROWING UP
RESPONSIBLY

L et's take another lesson from watching children
at play. Isn't this more fun than reading educational
books? Books about children are filled with words,
and words are rather dry. Child's play is filled with
laughter and tears—at least both of those have a little
moisture about them.

Have you ever noticed what children play? They
play at being parents; so they get the dolls out, dress
them, feed them, and put them to bed, and spank
them and love them.

They play at being at school. They designate students and teachers and get out the crayons and paper,
and they learn. (Have you ever been amazed at how
the child you almost have to bribe every morning to

get to school comes home after school and plays school?)

They play at board games. If they don't know the rules or even if they can't read the rules, no matter. They can just make up the rules as they go along.

They play at high finance; so they set up a lemonade stand out by the street.

Do you see a pattern in this? When children play, they play at being adults. Isn't that cute? Little imitators—always copying what they see us do. But isn't that also scary? Little imitators—always copying what they see us do.

> *We are born originals but die copies.*
> **EDWARD YOUNG**

The other day, I was with a group of seven adults having a barbecue in the back yard. A neighbor child, perhaps three years old, came over to the yard to visit the two-and-a-half-year-old. The little hostess, just barely in complete sentences herself, lined up the adults in a semi-circle and proceeded with proper introductions to her friend. She handled the whole situation with such poise and maturity that we almost forgot to be shocked by what was going on. It seemed so natural—this two-and-a-half-year-old doing introductions in an adult fashion.

But let's get beyond the simple explanations of this phenomenon as mere imitation. There may be something more profound at work here. It seems that in every child, regardless of the age, there is constant tension to flirt with what it means to be a grown-up.

> *Children are natural mimics—they act like their parents in spite of every attempt to teach them good manners.*
>
> **ANONYMOUS**

Okay. What's one of the first characteristics of being grown up?

"Responsibility," the masses shout.

"You've got work to do, and you've got children to raise. You've got important matters to settle. You have to assume some responsibility."

Now, let's put those last two observations together. If children want to experiment with being adults, and if one of the characteristics of being adult is responsibility, well, then, let's give them some responsibility. Doesn't that seem like a natural response to a normal need?

I say this fully aware that I may be about to get myself into trouble with some childrearing experts. There are those who tell us sad stories about children who are forced to grow up too soon without ever enjoying childhood. I recognize that danger. But it seems to me that giving your child normal responsibility and expecting him to carry it through is healthy.

Before you send a six-year-old out to clean the gutters and paint the eaves, let's be reasonable. There are ways to give a child a little taste of responsibility without stripping him of his dignity and the innocence of childhood. Let's look at these ways.

Responsibility by Involvement

The simplest way to give your child a share in the responsibility of the family is to tell him about it. I say this knowing the threat of sounding controversial. But I don't mind being controversial when I'm right! I have occasionally heard ministers yell at their congregation about the perils of bringing work home and robbing the family of its essence.

Fiddlesticks!

Work is part of the essence of the family. I feel sorry for those children who don't know what their parents do in the work world. Not to know what their parents do is not to know the parents—to be shut out of a major portion of their lives.

> It is NORMAL for a sixteen-year-old to show absolutely no interest in the parent's profession. It is also normal for that same child to enter the parent's profession ten years later.

It's not a coincidence that the first word all three of my children said with enough clarity to convince a non-relative that it really was a word was "football." I'm a football coach. I am not a maitre d' in a tea shop. When my children want to borrow the car or stay out past curfew, they need to know that I'm a coach. Life goes smoother when we both understand this.

I also feel sorry for the parents whose children don't know what they do. I know some parents who are rather good at their jobs. I think it would be sad to deny their children the opportunity to respect their parents at what they're good at.

> Sons are a heritage from the LORD,
>   children a reward from him.
> Like arrows in the hands of a warrior
>   are sons born in one's youth.
> Blessed is the man
>   whose quiver is full of them.
>   *Psalm 127:3-5*

So, how do we handle this little technique of involvement? We tell them. We make it the subject of the bedtime story. We talk around the dinner table. I suppose if we're really brave, we could take them to work with us like the father did in *Mary Poppins*.

Lest you think that I'm exaggerating, let me assure you that I'm serious. As I meet dozens of people's children every day, I am convinced that telling a child what you do for a living not only gives a child an opportunity for some satisfaction, but it's the first step in giving him some responsibility.

If you want to check the power in doing something like this, consider how many children go into their parent's professions. That, too, is a joyous and frightening statistic.

There is also another dimension to this business of involvement in responsibility, and that is the family budget.

I just don't understand why some parents choose not to involve their children in how the money is made. I also don't understand why some parents choose not to involve their children in where the money goes.

Of course, this doesn't have to be an elaborate lesson, nor does it have to come with a guilt-producing hidden nature. But involving our children in forming the budget could be a fun and educational family activity.

Educators are worried that we aren't providing our children with enough problem-solving activities. Try this as a math problem for your fifth-grader. Have her compute the cost of driving the automobile one mile. Not only will it provide her with some mental exercise, but you may be able to use her own statistics against her in a couple of years when she wants you to take her to the mall every night.

> **It is NORMAL for junior-high students to look at the shopping mall as a Temple of Mating Rituals.**

When parents of teenagers complain to me about their children abusing the telephone, I always ask if those culprits know how much it costs to operate a phone. That's a fair question. I would think that every young person ought to know the answer to it before he decides how long his calls should be.

Too often we accuse young people of being rude, irresponsible, and lazy when the major problem may be that they are just uninformed. Informing them is the first step to involvement, which is the first step to responsibility.

Responsibility by Consequence

If we were to ask those people who have to live with your children when you're not living with them (their teachers), "What is the most important lesson parents should teach their children before sending them out of the house?" what do you think you'd get for an answer?

Well, the first answer is rather obvious. "Teach them to use the bathroom," the teachers would say.

But the second answer is right up with that in popularity. "Teach them to accept the consequences of their own actions," teachers would shout en masse. Every day teachers shout that to me often and loudly.

We are living in a no-fault age. We have no-fault insurance, no-fault divorce, and no-fault felonies. The other day, I read a newspaper account of an accident. A man opened his car door on a busy city street. A policeman riding a horse came by, ran into the door, and knocked it off its hinges. The insurance paid for the car damages, calling the whole affair "an act of God." I believe in the sovereignty of God as much as the next person, but I have a hard time putting all this blame on God. I suspect that there was some human error involved somewhere; and if not human error, at least some horse error.

Our children seem to learn this no-fault concept fairly early. You can hear the language in the classroom.

"Who's whispering too loudly?" the teacher asks.
"It's not my fault," the guilty party answers.

"Why are you late for class?"
"It's not my fault."

"Why is your pencil sticking out of your nose?"
"It's not my fault."

The lesson of responsibility requires that we accept the hard, cruel reality that there are some events in this world that are *our fault.*

Maybe we can teach this attitude in a few simple principles.

"If you spill it, clean it up."
"If you break it, fix it."
"If you want it, work for it."
"If you start it, finish it."

But as simple as these principles sound, they're tough lessons to teach. They're probably tougher on the teacher than they are on the learner. When my son got into a little spat with the kids down on the corner, it took a lot of resolve to resist the temptation to run down and get involved myself. At a time like that, you have to be committed to the principle, "If you start it, finish it."

> **It is NORMAL for children of all ages to leave doors open. That includes refrigerator doors, car doors, and outside doors.**

Learning to accept the responsibility of your actions is an important lesson of growing—of living.

The Responsibility of Activity

Another way to teach your children a sense of responsibility is to put them to work. You may want to discourage full-time, forty-hours-a-week jobs until they are at least twelve or thirteen years of age (!), but you can find chores around the house for them to do. If it isn't practical for you to buy a cow and get some chickens, use your imagination. There are enough chores that have to be done around any normal home to involve every member of the household.

> **It is NORMAL for that adolescent who wouldn't even boil water at home to be an excellent employee when he works for the people down the street.**

You probably have two protests for this, one that you will admit to and one that you won't. Your first protest is that you don't want to give your child too many chores because you'll cheat him out of his play time. But then for his play time, you buy him a toy vacuum sweeper, toy dishes to wash, toy tools. Doesn't it seem reasonable that if he gets a kick out of pushing the toy, he'll get a kick out of pushing the real thing? If children are going to play at chores, they may as well do chores.

Now, consider the protest you probably won't admit to. The real reason most of us don't have our children involved in chores as much as we could is that we don't have the patience to teach them how. Let's face it. It's easier to wash the dishes yourself than it is to teach your child. So, we cheat our children out of the valuable lesson of responsibility, and we cheat ourselves out of some good help because we don't have the patience to teach or to accept a job not done as well as we could do it.

But beyond the obvious lesson in this responsibility by activity is an even deeper, more profound and valuable lesson—the lesson of feeling worthwhile through usefulness.

That's the topic for the next chapter.

7

FEELING
WORTHWHILE

L et's begin with a rather simple question. Do you do your best work when you are feeling depressed, despondent, insecure, or non-worthwhile? Probably not. Most people don't, and that includes our children. Thus, if we are going to expect our children to work up to their normal capacities, we have to do what we can to make sure they feel that they are worthwhile and capable of achieving something.

Of course, this isn't news. We have been bombarded with the language even before we began to comtemplate bringing children into the world and embarking on this risk-filled trek called parenthood.

Unless we hide in the cellar, at least once a day we are going to get some exposure—either from a new book, a television talk show, or a radio call-in program—about something called self-esteem, self-concept, positive mental attitude, self-image or even a healthy sense of worthwhileness.

By now you have surely heard so much about this topic that you are either bored to tears with the whole subject or you are scared to death—or maybe you are a little of both. And I don't blame you. So why am I bringing it up now? You have already heard the experts, and you have heard them so often that you could give their speeches for them in your sleep. What more do I have to contribute to the issue?

Not much really. But as a teacher, I believe in the instructional value of repetition. And this is a lesson we have to learn.

Regardless of how bored we may be and regardless of what we may think of the topic, we still have to face the reality. Somebody in this world needs to have enough confidence in himself to think that he can at least do the job at hand.

> **It is NORMAL for any child of any age to think that she is not bright enough, not pretty enough, not talented enough, or not popular enough.**

If no one in the whole world thought he was capable of writing a book, there would be no new books. We wouldn't have to cut down trees to make paper. The forests would take over the world, and birds would lose their minds trying to decide where to roost. What a mess!

If no one thought he was capable of making a speech, there would be no speeches made. (Surely, there is some reason why this wouldn't be good.)

If no one thought that he was capable of learning to play a musical instrument, there would be no music, and parents and children would have one less issue to fight about. Besides, who wants to live in a world without music?

If no one thought he was any good in sports, there would be no baseball, and grown-up people who play the game would not have a good excuse for acting like little children.

If no student thought he was capable of learning the material in class, no one would make an A; and that bell-shaped curve would look like a balloon blown too full.

Somewhere, somehow, someone must get enough of a sense of worth to know that he is capable of achieving something worthwhile.

> "Be strong and courageous. Do not be terrified; do not be discouraged, for the LORD your God will be with you wherever you go."
>
> *Joshua 1:9*

That's why I'm not afraid to take a chance of repeating something you already know. I do it out of self-defense. My world works better when your child knows that he is capable.

For that reason, I present the following reminders.

Three Observations I Have Made Just by Standing around the Halls of Schools

#1 Insecurity rarely looks like insecurity.

Sometimes you see an insecure child or maybe an insecure adolescent, or maybe even an insecure adult, and you just whisper to yourself, "Well, that one is insecure." In other words, with some folks you can tell.

But on the other hand, there are times when insecurity isn't all that obvious. Through the years, I have been fooled so many times that I have learned that I don't always know.

For example, I helped sponsor a party for eighth-graders. The host suggested that these young people play a new game he had planned just for the occasion. The response was expected. They shouted in unison, "We don't want to play that dumb game. Let's play something fun like basketball." The host demanded that they play the new game. Pouting and complaining, those eighth-graders played the game, but with the definite explanation that they were only following orders. They hated it.

But about twenty minutes later when the host told them that they could now play basketball, in unison they shouted, "No, we want to play this game all evening." Now, why couldn't these people have said from the very beginning that they were reluctant to play the new game because they were insecure about it? Why did they have to camouflage their insecurity behind a mask of apathy? But this is the way people often work. Their masks of insecurity come in a variety of styles.

In every fifth-grade Sunday-school class in the whole world there is surely one special child. I have heard about this person from Sao Paulo to Manitoba, so I know he exists and I know that he exists in abundance. This child is the designated problem child, the legend of the whole church. He can't sit still. He can't keep his hand off other people. He always interrupts. In short, he hates Sunday school and he is making a lot of other people hate it, too—especially the teacher.

"So what's so unusual?" you ask. "I have seen lots of those kinds of people before."

Well, the thing that makes this person so amazing is that we discover that he really doesn't act this way anywhere else. In school he is a well-behaved person who plays by the rules.

What's the problem? None of us likes to be put into places where we are going to look stupid. Most of us resist those places as often as we can, but when we find ourselves thrust into a situation, we create some means of coping.

Children are masters at this. There is a good chance that such a child is just trying to hide his feeling that he is not as capable in this Sunday-school arena as the other students. Thus, he wears a mask to hide his insecurity.

I could go on all day with these kinds of stories because we see them all the time—the mask of bragging, the mask of laziness, the mask of being a bully, the mask of arrogance, the mask of aloofness—the many masks of insecurity, but you get the point.

#2 It is normal to feel inferior.

The other day, I had a long conversation with a fourteen-year-old high-school freshman who read at about the fifth-grade level. And he knew it. Several well-meaning people had pointed it out to him— teachers, counselors, reading specialists, and even his parents. In the course of the hour or so we spent together, his perspective took on a hint of bitter futility. The night before, the young man had been required by a teacher to watch a television documentary on the plight of the functionally illiterate American. As a result, the young man was having some feelings of inferiority.

Recently, I had a long conversation with a high-school senior who had just been named basketball queen at her school. She is one of the top students, a cheerleader, sings in the swing choir, and has now won a popularity contest by being named queen. During our conversation, her perspective took on a hint of bitter futility. Her brother had just won a huge scholarship to study engineering at a prestigious university. She was pleased for her brother but she felt pressure from her parents to achieve at least as much as he had. That young lady was having some feelings of inferiority.

Some time ago, I had a conversation with a middle-aged teacher who had just won a state award for the quality of his teaching. But instead of talking about the honor the man told me all the ways he had failed to be the kind of teacher he wanted to be this year. That man was having some feelings of inferiority.

One day, God went to a very talented man and said, "I need you to lead my people out of that horrible bondage in Egypt to the Promised Land." But that man, named Moses, thought of a number of reasons why that wasn't such a good idea. That talented man, too, was having some feelings of inferiority.

> *'Tis an old saw, Children and fools speak true.*
>
> **JOHN SEYLY**

I conclude with that final illustration for two reasons. I want to reemphasize the point that *it is normal to feel inferior.* Maybe I know all the wrong people in the world, or maybe all the people who have enough spare time to do nothing better than get acquainted with me are different. But everybody I know struggles with feelings of inferiority—often seriously limiting and even debilitating feelings of inferiority. So apparently it's normal, and we need to admit that. Sometimes we just need to say to ourselves, "Well, I feel just like Moses must have felt when God gave him that enormous assignment."

We also need to realize that these feelings are common in our children, even during those times when we may not see them.

> **It is NORMAL for a small baby to cry at night and sleep during the day. Come to think of it, that's normal for a fifteen-year-old, too.**

But the second reason we need to look at this illustration is that it does teach us that those feelings of inferiority are unwarranted, particularly when we are in the hands of an omnipotent and omniscient God.

> When I was woven together in the
>   depths of the earth,
>   your eyes saw my unformed body.
> All the days ordained for me
>   were written in your book
>   before one of them came to be.
> *Psalm 139:15-16*

#3 A feeling of worth in rearing children involves two people.

We have libraries of materials telling us about the issue of self-esteem in our children. Although I am glad for the material, and I do find it helpful, all this discussion about self-esteem in children needs to begin with some discussion about self-esteem in the parent. The two work in harmony.

We can read the books, develop the devices, and employ the methods just as we are told to do, but if we don't think we ourselves are worth much, surely our children won't think much of themselves either.

For all of our scientific analysis of the subject, feeling worthy has the characteristic of being contagious. We catch it from each other.

Methods for Developing a Sense of Worth

I present this next section with much fear. Every book and every speaker gives you another list of specific methods to follow moment by moment and day by day so that you will have enough confidence to get out of bed, get dressed, and confront life. Also, every book and every speaker gives you a list to follow in helping your child develop his self-image sufficiently to succeed in the world. I can't contribute anything new to that list, so let me summarize what you have already been told. Basically, I think that all the methods can be put into two general categories. Let's look at these.

#1 We can try to prove that we are worthy.

That sounds simple enough and rather wholesome. If you want to develop enough sense of worth to be able to accomplish your objectives for this day, you can just go about proving to yourself that you are worthy.

But how do you prove it? Well, that's simple, too. You can beat somebody up. Let me repeat that lest you didn't hear it the first time. YOU CAN BEAT SOMEBODY UP. You can just choose somebody, take him out behind the barn, and punch his face in.

Surely I jest. I wouldn't advocate violence. But I'll bet I did get your attention. Now, just to make this fun, let's use that idea of beating somebody up as a symbol—a metaphor, as the poets would say. Let's use it as a metaphor for competition. And actually, that's rather the spirit of competition, isn't it? To beat somebody up?

Regardless of how much we may want to protest, competition is the common device for proving that we are worthy. We beat people out for the job. We beat somebody to the parking spot. We win the big game. We win the music contest. We play first chair in the band. We are the first in line. We get the highest grade on the test. Our finger painting is voted best. We are voted the basketball queen. We get the lead role in the play.

Have you ever noticed how many of our achievements are based on the fact that for us to achieve, somebody has to lose? So we may as well admit that we are beating others up because that is what we are really doing, isn't it?

I know that this sounds harsh, but I wanted it to sound harsh. I want us all to take a long, hard look at what happens when most of us set out to prove that we are worth something.

This common method, which so many of us use, has drawbacks. For one thing, it's fickle. Sometimes we don't do the beating, but instead we are beat upon. And when that happens we go through those old feelings of inferiority all over again.

Proving ourselves worthy is a never-ending activity. We have to do it continuously. When competition is the only real method we offer our children, they must live with the pressure every moment of every day, and they must live in constant peril of losing their confidence.

Let's see if possibly there is a better way. We will call that category two.

#2 *We can just know that we are worthy.*
If you don't want to wear yourself out every day going around beating people up, you might be able to eliminate all the effort by just deciding that you don't really need to do that. Decide on your own that you are of great worth, and you don't really need to try to prove it to anyone.

But let me caution you. This is largely an untried method. Most of us still rely on the old beating-people-up routine. But I do think that this new idea is worth some thought.

As we work through a system of applying this to our children, let's go back to that earlier idea that we parents must first work out our own feelings of worth even before we tackle the problem with our children.

Can we just accept the fact that we are worthy? Without being arrogant or boastful, would it be all right to admit that we are fairly decent at this business of being parents? Of course there are times when we have some doubts.

Maybe the child complains for a week about a pain in his hand. We finally break down and take him to the doctor to discover that there is a broken bone after all. It does make you feel like something of a loser, doesn't it? That becomes one of those incidents that isn't too funny until about twenty years later.

The teacher calls you in to tell you that your child is (take your pick):

A. Not performing at class level.
B. Starving for attention and love.
C. The class clown.
D. An embarrassment.
E. All of the above.

As you sit in that student desk during that discussion, you had better hope you can just know that you are a fairly decent parent because at that particular moment, you won't be able to think of any way to prove it.

Perhaps the police call you to come down and bail out your adolescent. *Whoops!* Maybe we weren't supposed to be that realistic here. After all, we are talking about normal children and normal families. Maybe you will never have to do this. Maybe your child will never be picked up for speeding, reckless driving, riding in an automobile with an open container, buying drugs. But at least try imagining the situation. The activity will be good for you and it will help you identify with us parents who have been through it. Do you have any way of convincing yourself that you are fairly good at being a parent during those moments when everybody around you is doubting it?

Of course you do, if you stop to think about it. God picked you to be the parent of this child. He hand-picked you for some special reason. God, with infinite wisdom, chose *you.* Now what more proof do you want? Say to yourself, "God picked me, and all the time he knew the mistakes I would make. But there is a reason for this. So I think I'll celebrate. I'm a fairly decent parent."

After we have accepted for ourselves that lesson, we are now ready to begin to teach it to our child. "God picked you to be my child. God gave you those eyes, those dimples, that hair. You are a fairly decent person because God made you that way."

Maybe I'm just dreaming. Maybe this won't work at all. Maybe we ought to forget all this foolishness and just have our child go beat somebody up. I do know that this second method is harder. If we are going to make it work, we have to have those conversations with our child about a dozen times a day—a hundred times a day if our child is in the seventh grade. We have to work constantly at reminding the child of his worth.

> **It is NORMAL for ninth-graders to be tardy for class. It is also normal that one or all of the following excuses could be accurate.**
>
> • **My locker stuck.**
> • **I had to go to the bathroom.**
> • **The teacher kept me after class.**
> • **I saw my counselor in the hall.**
> • **My friend was crying.**
> • **I fell down the stairs.**
> • **I dropped my pencil.**
> • **I got yelled at for running in the hall.**
> • **It's too far to come.**

But I think it is worth the effort. Hanging around the halls of schools and observing other people's children has turned me into something of an optimist. I have seen some amazing transformations, and I have learned that it's never too late.

I met James when he was a ninth-grader, and even then, he was doomed to a life of failure and despair. He wasn't a vicious person. He just never took anything seriously. He had no vision of a future, so he made the most of now, and the purpose of now was to have fun. Somehow he managed to get involved in every piece of mischief in the whole school for the next three years. I will never know where he got all the energy. But mischief is time consuming, so James never quite got around to the more mundane things like homework and studying. His grades were dismal. But in spite of all this, I liked James. He had personality, style, and energy.

> *Children have more need of models than of critics.*
>
> **JOSEPH JOUBERT**

On the day before he was to start his senior year, James came to see me. He asked a strange question: Did I think he had the natural ability to be a fair student? In other words, he had real feelings of inferiority. In all honesty, I could answer that I thought he had the ability. James sat there, contemplated all this for a bit, and decided to commit himself to trying. He finished his senior year with almost all "A"s, went to college where he made excellent grades, and now is teaching at a university.

Another man I know realized at twenty-two years of age that he couldn't read yet because of his own feeling of insecurity. At that age, he began the tedious trek of teaching himself to read, and from that he has gone on to become a very successful businessman.

Those stories are just for starters. I tell them as a method of offering some assurance. I don't think that we can learn the lesson by just telling ourselves that we are worthwhile. But we do have to learn patience. Neither we, nor our children, might believe it the first time we hear it said; but if we assure ourselves often enough, maybe someday we can even prove that we are worthwhile—and do it without any violence.

8

THE URGE TO CREATE

In recent years, I have been making progress in discovering a new scientific breakthrough. I have been working on an antidote for seriousness. And I think I am on to something.

About the time the business meeting gets too deep with charts, graphs, and reports of losses without enough balance with profits, about the time the sermon gets too theological with Greek roots and endings all over the place, about the time tension reaches a climax, someone stops and tells a personal family story. That seems to have wonderful therapeutic value, both for the teller and for the listener. But I do suspect that the secret is that when someone tells a personal family story, we all become something of tellers because we all have families and to have families is to tell a family story. I think the experts call that active listening.

But it seems to work. Bill Cosby made more money than a major corporation telling us stories about a normal family doing normal things. Anybody who has any family at all knows that there was nothing created and invented there (except for the made beds). It was typical stuff, but we needed it to bring some relief to all the seriousness that often creeps in and stirs us up.

I have learned the worth of this within the family itself. I'm going to share with you this technique on the promise that you will never tell my wife Mary.

Once in a while, when I come home from a busy day at work, I get the sense that things are too serious as I walk through the door. Tension is not an abstract noun. At our house, tension is concrete: it can be heard, felt, tasted, smelled, and seen with the naked eye. But the cause of tension at our house is always easy to locate. I have goofed up somewhere. I forgot to take out the trash. I forgot that it was our anniversary. I forgot to make the house payment. I took the children somewhere and I forgot and left one of them. Regardless of the reason, all of a sudden, I am overwhelmed with seriousness. This calls for quick thinking and an effective antidote.

At that point, just as the storm is about to break loose, wreaking havoc on my peace, I smile and say to Mary, "Have you talked to our two-year-old grand-daughter today?"

It works like a wonder drug. She gives me a twen-ty-minute definition of today's cuteness, and the storm clouds roll by our house once more. I give you this technique free of charge. If you find it as effective for you as it is for me, you can send a contribution to my favorite mission organization in appreciation.

But I bring all this up to make another point. I had begun to feel that this whole discussion about raising normal children had begun to get a little too serious. That means that it is time to stop and tell some personal family stories. They may not have any other point, but they should work as tension-busters.

Family Stories

When our son was two years old, he went through a stage of thinking that he was a dog. He walked around on all fours; he sniffed our pant legs, and he wanted to eat his meals from a bowl on the floor. At first, all of this bothered us a bit until we found a way to let him be happy and make a profit at the same time. We rented him out to the bird hunters.

I just made that last part up. We really didn't rent him out. But we did enjoy his being a pet for us. And I think he must have been fairly convincing in his imaginative state. At least he convinced other dogs. For a period of about a year, our son played with every ferocious animal in the neighborhood and never once was bitten or harmed. Now, how do you explain that?

Our daughter, sometime in her childhood, became best friends with an imaginary child. This child, named Fricka, lived with us for a couple of years. And she was one of the worst kids I have ever been around. She was always spilling milk, eating the last cookie, not making her bed, causing too much noise at night. And she didn't take orders as well as our pet dog (our son) did. Of course, she didn't eat much and never used up much water taking showers, so I guess there was *something* positive about her.

But if you think that imagination is something, you should know my wife. She imagines that she is Mario Andretti. When she takes out the family station wagon for a spin on the freeway, she puts on her goggles and helmet and drives about 180 miles per hour. And every time she passes a car, she mutters something that sounds remotely like, "Eat my dust, Mac. Eat my dust."

The Possibilities Are Endless

Isn't imagination wonderful? That's one of the great promises of being a parent of a normal child. You get a front-row seat to watch imagination in full bloom. Of course, for you with your particular child, it's even better because surely your child is the cutest and most imaginative child around, except for my wife's granddaughter.

> **It is NORMAL for a child to walk through
> a puddle, even if he has to go out of his
> way to find it.**

By now, you are probably rather excited about the possibilities proposed here. At least if you are normal, you are a little excited.

All this talk about imagination has become exciting stuff recently. We hear experts talk about the need for helping our children master such things as critical-thinking skills and problem-solving skills, and we get excited. We may not even be too sure what those things are or how they work with our children, but we do know that they are something worth having.

Of course, when our children master those skills and turn them against us, we take another look. For example, when our sixteen-year-old uses his best courtroom logic to persuade us that he should have full use of the family car next Saturday night, we might actually wonder why we were so excited about his critical thinking in the first place. Maybe that isn't what the educators are talking about when they talk about noble virtues.

When we hear of imagination, we also begin to think in terms of creativity, and that talk excites us. As parents, we are all concerned that our children preserve that childlike urge to create, so we read everything we can get our hands on about the rich expressions and artistic abilities implicit in finger painting. In the meantime we check out books to read

about all the techniques we can use to assure ourselves that our child can write a Pulitzer Prize-winning
novel when he is eight years old. All we have to do is
help him cultivate his imagination.

Well, that does sound like exciting stuff, and I really
do wish I could get into the discussion. But unfor-
tunately, I can't. I just want to talk about imagination.
No problem-solving skills, no creativity, no finger
painting fit to be hung in the Louvre, no prize-winning
novels. Just imagination. Just thinking that you are
a dog, or imagining that you have a make-believe
friend.

I am not trying to turn a child's imagination into
something profitable or brilliant; that's what perfect
parents of perfect children do. We're just talking about
being normal. And at that level, I want to celebrate the
full range of the imagination running free and even
wild if it wants to. The normal child may never create
a thing, but at least he still needs his imagination.

Party Rules

Since I have now invited you to this celebration, let
me give you some rules for the party.

#1 Imagination is fun.
In fact, imagination is about the cheapest form of
entertainment there is, unless of course, the child
imagines that he is a bird and tries to fly off the roof
or something.

Emily Dickinson is one of my favorite poets for at least a couple of reasons. For one thing, she wrote short poems and you can read them without staying awake late at night wondering how they are going to come out. But the other reason I like her poetry is that she seems to understand the sheer joy of imagination, of a child's imagination if you please.

In one poem she writes:

"There is no frigate like a book
To take us miles away."

Of course, she said some other things in that poem as well, but that's about as much as I can remember. But it is enough to give us the point. Do you see what can be made from two simple ingredients—an active imagination and a book? Or an imagination and a box? Or an imagination and a stick?

> **It is NORMAL for children to enjoy the box more than the toy.**
> **Moral: Give empty boxes for Christmas.**

I had a favorite stick when I was a boy. Because he had some blotches where the bleach had spilled on him, I named him Spot. I put a piece of twine around his head and I rode him all over the countryside. But he was a multi-talented stick. I even entered him in the Kentucky Derby once. He won, of course. Now, I haven't ever been to the Kentucky Derby in real life;

but if I ever get there, I doubt that I will be too surprised. After all, I won it once, riding a bleach-dyed stick named Spot. I don't know what ever happened to old Spot, but he did eat less food than a real horse would have.

This is the joy of imagination. When your father won't let you have a horse, you can create one!

When children stand quiet, they have done some ill.

GEORGE HERBERT

In recent years I've heard grownups speak with serious dismay that our young people no longer have heroes, and we despair at what this means. Perhaps they haven't learned the lesson of respect or perhaps there isn't anyone worthy of their respect.

Well, I don't know the answer to all those heady moral questions, but I know something about another dimension of having a hero. Having a hero is more than having a hero. Carried to its extreme in the imagination, it is *becoming*. When I was growing up, Alvin Dark was my hero, but to say it that way is an understatement. I became Alvin Dark. When we played baseball out in the pasture behind the barn, I was really Alvin Dark. I walked like him. When I batted, I used his same glare. If I ever hit the ball, I took that wide turn at first base and dared them to throw behind me so I could go to second.

Maybe the concern with our children nowadays is more than just a question of heroes. Maybe in there somewhere is the question of the imagination.

I think that I am supposed to stop here and mourn the death of imagination. Somehow we have killed it and because of that we are cheating our children out of the great joys of childhood.

Maybe it was television that did it. Television is a good culprit to blame for the ills of society. Maybe our children just sit there in a catatonic stupor, engrossed in beads flashing across the screen, and have become so entranced that they have lost the art and joy of imagination.

Or maybe it was Little League that committed this felony. After all, it's pretty tough to imagine that you are Alvin Dark when you are wearing a seventy-dollar uniform, batting with thirty-dollar gloves on each hand, playing before five-hundred people, and knowing that your time at bat decides the city championship.

Maybe all that is true, but honestly, I don't know whether it is or not. I don't know if children use their imaginations as much or less than we did. Imagination is such a personal thing. It's my dreams and my thoughts, and I very rarely share those with anyone else. I have no idea what anyone else is imagining unless he tells me. So I just can't contribute to this search for the killer because I don't know whether it's dead or not.

The one thing that I *have* noticed is that when Mary puts on her helmet and goggles and goes 180 miles per hour down the freeway, our daughter Kris sits in the front passenger's seat, puckers up her lips, and blows that sound like a well-tuned motor humming perfectly. And at twenty-two years old, Kris is still doing that.

#2 Imagination needs respect.

Although I don't know whether imagination is dead or not, I do know that we adults who hang around in a child's space can certainly contribute to it by just showing the work of imagination a little respect. Let me mention again that we are making a distinction between imagination and creativity. We probably get rather excited about reinforcing our child's creative urges, particularly when they look like what we would expect them to look like. But we may not be that cognizant or respectful of simple works of an imaginative mind.

> **It's NORMAL for a child to have a higher appreciation of food art than the adults at the table do.**

But it wouldn't hurt us. When I was a boy I never told anybody about my relationship with Alvin Dark.

I guess there might have been a few clues. I had my room papered with posters. I kept his batting average posted on my door. I wore his team's cap every day. Little signs, I guess. But when my dad pitched to me out in that makeshift ball diamond behind the barn, he would sometimes say things like, "Let me see you hit this one, Alvin," and then he would grin. Maybe he knew all the time. But that's what fathers are for, to understand their children's imaginations.

Understanding imagination requires a bit of commitment. When that child calls you into his room at two o'clock in the morning to report a monster on the loose, you need to understand the power of imagination. Imagination always takes authority over reason. Imagined monsters are far more real than logical monsters. If a child tells you there is a monster in his room, you really ought to listen to that child at that particular moment. Why? Because that monster is as real as the pain in his hand that turned out to be a broken bone a week later when you got around to taking him to the doctor.

As Emily Dickinson tells us in her poem, the abilities to create images in our minds from the printed word and to be where we have never been before are wonderful abilities that deserve our respect.

#3 Imagination needs freedom.
If our children are going to enjoy the full use of their imaginations, they will require a bit of freedom. That

is a tough order because providing them some freedom often requires something of a commitment on our
part.

Whoever welcomes a little child like
this in my name welcomes me.
Matthew 18:5

For example, imagination often requires some freedom of time. In other words, imagination may get in
the way of getting the chores finished. I had a daughter
like that. For her, there were always two time expec-
tancies. There was my time, the *now*, and there was
the time her imagination needed. I would say with the
matter-of-fact confidence of a parent in charge of his
little world, "Clean up your room."

When I went back an hour later and could see no
change, I would say, in tones that indicated I was now
a little less in charge, "Didn't I tell you to clean up your
room?"

She would answer, in tones of a little girl in charge
of things, "Well, I am cleaning it up. I have all the dolls
ready for bed." Obviously, there are two different
concepts of time at work here. Mine, and the one we
are going to go by.

Imagination might even require, dare we say it, a
little daydreaming; and as everyone knows, daydreaming is to be discouraged. Have you ever stopped

to count the number of times we reprimand a child for daydreaming?

> "If you hadn't been daydreaming in class, you would have known what the assignment is."
> "If I catch you daydreaming in church again, I am going to make you start taking notes."
> "Don't daydream while I am talking to you."

But I'm not sure daydreaming is the terrible activity we make it out to be. Some of the times I have been proudest of my children and happiest with my work as a parent were when they could daydream. Something would happen and I would have to leave them in the car alone for half an hour while I conducted business. But they would always assure me that they weren't bored. Or, for the acid test, I would take them to the doctor's office for that endless wait in the lobby with all those old magazines, and they would sit still.

But daydreaming works on its own timetable. We may have to accept that.

Children are God's small interpreters.
WHITTIER

Imagination also requires some freedom of space or, if not freedom of space, at least freedom from ridicule. In other words, imaginative people frequently talk to

themselves. Now, talking to oneself is perfectly accept-
able behavior, except to the people who don't talk to
themselves. It also gives full range to an active imagination because it allows the imagination to take on
the concrete reality of oral language.

Not only that, the habit is good training for those
people who plan on becoming novelists, or poets, or
playwrights, or lighthouse keepers, or shepherds. (I
was going to add ministers to that list, but I am not
sure I remember why.)

The problem, though, arises when a self-entertainer
(how about that term? I just made it up to describe
those special people) must live in a house somewhere
in the suburbs with five others, none of whom has
mastered the art. Detection is often and almost always
humiliating.

And there is nothing more embarrassing than for
one of those special people to be caught right in the
middle of a good conversation wth himself. Although
those moments could provide some humor for the rest
of the family, that kind of surveillance could go a long
way in hampering someone's imagination.

And we don't want to do that. Although imagination
does require a bit of unusual freedom of circumstances, it is still worth the effort. Imagination is not
only *normal*, but it is the device by which the normal
can turn life into something beautiful and extraordi-
nary.

It has earned our celebration.

9
LIKE IS PART OF
LOVE

I went to see a gymnastics meet, and as usual the activities in the stands were more educational than those on the floor. I like gymnastics, really I do. I applaud the combination of strength, skill, and grace.

But I also enjoy watching human beings doing human things. They are such fascinating animals—so individual and so predictable.

On this particular day, a man came down and sat near me. He was accompanied by his son who seemed to be about four or five years old. He was a cute boy with clear blue eyes, a little cowlick in his blond hair, and a pleasant smile.

But I'm not sure the father saw all that. He was more concerned with the boy's behavior than his looks, and the boy's behavior was definitely within the range of normal. He wiggled in his seat, tore up his program, gulped his Coke, turned and stared at the people behind them, and in general acted normal.

Father was obviously upset by all this. He scowled, scolded, threatened, and eventually, with a flush of anger, moved three rows down so he would not be interrupted by that four-year-old.

As the meet progressed, it became obvious that the father had another son who was one of the athletes competing. During a break in the action, that son came up into the stands to chat with his dad. He, too, was a handsome young man, about fifteen years old, and he was doing well in the meet.

But I couldn't believe Dad when the older boy came up. It was as if a new person I had never seen before had come while I wasn't looking. He was cordial to his son; he spoke calmly and grinned; and on several occasions, he touched the boy with reassuring gestures.

> *You save an old man and you save a unit, but you save a boy and you save a multiplication table.*
>
> **GIPSY SMITH**

Now, how do you explain the difference? Maybe moving two rows down allowed his sinuses to clear up so he felt better. Maybe he thought the television cameras were on when the athlete was in the stands, and he was auditioning for a McDonald's commercial.

And maybe there's another explanation—one that is far too common in the Dad business. Just maybe this father liked his older son more than he liked his younger son. At least, on that day.

But you protest. "How can you measure a father's love? You can't stick a thermometer in his mouth and get much of a reading."

But I fooled you. I am not talking about love. I'm talking about like, and the two are definitely different. In an earlier section of the book, I asked you if your child knows that you love him. (Notice how I worked this in as a gentle reminder. I do hope you remember; but if you don't, don't panic. You're just being normal.) I hope I phrased that original point in such language that you at least did a quick analysis of yourself and slipped into the appropriate degree of guilt.

But now, we ask an even tougher question. *Do you like your child?*

I rarely question parents' love. As a teacher, I am supposed to say, "Parents don't care about their kids anymore. That's what's wrong with this world. That's why I can't teach. That's why I have bunions and a sore back." That speech is part of the teacher catechism, to be memorized in teacher school and recited during every bad day you ever have, and on especially bad days, recited every period.

But I don't believe it. Almost all the parents I know care and care deeply about their children, how they act and what happens to them. I think that parents love their children. That's normal.

> It is **NORMAL** for a nine-year-old not to enjoy sitting in plastic school chairs for six-hour blocks of time. Normal reactions to these conditions might include squirming, shuffling, squealing, punching, poking, and provoking, any of which might be severe enough to draw reprimands from the adults in charge who may or may not have to sit in plastic chairs.

But liking your child is a different matter.

Like is a special component of love, so it is quite possible to love and not like. I see that all the time. That father with the two sons probably loved both of them about equally. But his like for them was obviously not equal, and that showed.

The experts have written some excellent books on loving your child. So even if I did know something about that subject, I probably couldn't add anything new.

Consequently, in this book for normal people doing normal things, we will focus our attention on that special component of like. Let's consider the characteristics.

The Characteristics of Like

Like likes being close.

You can love somebody and not spend a whole lot of time with that person. People my age casually tell me that they haven't seen their own parents for two years. But they love their parents. Fathers can be out of town on business for weeks at a time and still love their children. Husbands and wives can be separated for some reason, yet still love each other.

Sometimes people miss not being with the person they love, but others can love deeply and not miss the other person all that much. In fact, I know of some relationships where the love is a little stronger when the two don't spend so much time together.

But when you add the component of like, you change that. People who like each other like being close. They like to talk, to see each other, to breathe on each other. They like sharing mutual thoughts, participating in the same activities, and basking in the same moments.

Situations may cause them to be apart, but they don't enjoy it. When they are not close to the person they like, there is an abyss, a black hole in their being. A part of them is missing.

To give this idea a concrete image, let me use a personal story. I like my son. I like his sense of humor; I like his perspective; I like the way he breathes.

But my son lives 1100 miles away. I don't like that. I miss him. Unless you like someone as much as I like my son, you are not going to appreciate him like I do. I have encouraged my son, 1100 miles away, to subscribe to TV cable so that he and I can watch the same baseball game. When the game is over, I call him, and we bask in the moments together. There are other baseball fans closer than 1100 miles away, but none sees the game with the same perspective as my son. I like him.

To check out this concept of like, let's take a little test. The other day, I had to drive 900 miles—in a small automobile that ranges in comfort somewhere between awful and criminal—and it doesn't have a radio.

If you had to travel 900 miles in an uncomfortable car, whom would you like to take?

First, make a list of five people. Now rank those from one to five. In that whole list, did you have one of your children? How near the top?

That's what I am talking about with this business of like.

When I made the trip, I took my daughter. I like her. I like the way she looks at the countryside. We didn't fight. We didn't grow weary of each other. We like each other now even more because we made the trip together.

Like can be learned.
Based on what I read in Paul's letters, I believe that love can be learned, too—but it may be controversial

in some circles to say that, and I don't want to be controversial. So I will avoid argument by just arguing that like can be learned.

Of course, there could be some who would argue with that. I have met a wide variety of adolescents who don't seem to buy it. When you ask them why they picked some person for a friend, they just shrug and grunt, "I don't know (normal adolescents say that frequently). I just like him."

> **It is NORMAL for an early adolescent to resist any attempts to hug him and cry three days later because you don't ever hug him anymore.**

But from a parent's point, since we are the adults in the relationship, we can, through a minimum amount of heartache and discipline, learn to like.

One reason for that is that like is often age-related. Love isn't. If we are normal parents, we love our children through all sorts of escapades and stages. We love them as babies, as growing children, as adolescents, and as adults. But if we are honest, we will probably admit that sometimes it's a little harder to love them than at other times.

That's the issue of like. Some people just like people at one stage of development more than they like people at another.

For example, some teachers teach first grade and would quit the profession if they had to teach fourth grade.

Some doctors doctor babies and would quit the profession if they had to doctor adolescents.

Some parents love being parents to eight-year-olds and feel like quitting the profession when they have to parent middle-school people.

To get from infancy to adulthood, your child has to hit every stage. He can't skip over any. At times, you may feel like locking him away while he travels through a certain stage, but that wouldn't be nice. It would be more reasonable to lock yourself away during that time.

> **It's NORMAL for seniors to goof off the last quarter. That doesn't just apply to high-school seniors; it's even worse in college seniors.**

The other alternative is to learn to like a child at that stage. Of course you can do it.

The first step is to figure out what's normal for a person at that age. That way, you're not as surprised by the surprises.

There are several sources for that kind of information. You can read *Parents Magazine*, you can chat with teachers, or you can talk with other parents who are just as surprised as you are.

Now that you have all that information about how a person that age is supposed to act, the next step is to spend time with your child.

Let me assure you that I am serious. I have seen this technique work. If you don't like a person very much, you really need to spend more time with him.

As you get to know this person better, you will begin to see the special features, understand the perspective, and appreciate the situation. And the first thing you know, there is a like relationship established.

I heartily recommend this method. When you are honest enough with yourself to sense that your like for your child has begun to slip, take charge of the relationship. Learn as much as you can about this person, and just spend time with him.

In a child is the ability to forget a sorrow.
PHYLLIS McGINLEY

"But," you ask, "what happens if the chasm is already deep and wide? We haven't had a good relationship for a long while." Well, I think the method is still worth a try. I know of a family where father and son didn't speak to each other for two years. Then one day both of them learned something about like and now they are good friends. The message here is obvious.

Don't give up on the possibility of learning to like.

Like doesn't mean being equal.

Lurking somewhere in the concept of like is the idea of friendship. That's a reasonable use of language. But sometimes we get a mistaken notion of friendship. We get the idea that friends are always equals, but that doesn't have to be true. Two people can be friends, can like each other in a friendly way, and yet play two altogether different roles in the relationship.

> **It is NORMAL for thirteen-year-olds to stand on their toes and say to their shortest parent, "Look, I'm as tall as you are."**

Parents and children are not equals, regardless of how old the children may be. There is something altogether natural and normal about asking children to honor their parents. This is a biblical mandate.

> Listen, my sons, to a father's instruction; pay attention and gain understanding.
>
> *Proverbs 4:1*

But the mandate doesn't say that the two can't be friends or can't like each other. There can still be like and honor.

Actually, I offer this observation with a hint of warning: *As adults, we can never be our children's age again. There is no need to try. Our children know the difference, and they expect us to act our age.*

But they still appreciate it if we would like them.

Like shares in the fun.

Well, that's such an exciting possibility that maybe we ought to devote a whole chapter to it. And we will—the next one.

10
A HEALTHY DOSE OF LAUGHTER

If you want to be the proper parent of a normal child, you really need to try to live as long as you can. In other words, you need to take care of yourself. You need to do something in the name of your health.

You could eat healthy foods. But about the time you get your menu planned, they change the rules about what's healthy and what isn't. You could suffer semi-terminal stress just trying to decide what to do with all that oat bran in the cupboard.

You could get some exercise. But about the time you get your running shoes bought, they change the rules about what's good for you and what isn't. You could suffer semi-terminal nausea just trying to decide which exercise video you want to watch.

Good for You

So let me recommend a surefire, always-healthy activity that won't endanger your life in the process. For a good stimulant, try laughter.

I'm quite serious. As the experts say, "The research shows . . . " laughter is really very good for us. It causes the heart to beat, the blood to flow, and the juices to work. One fellow healed himself of a life-threatening illness just by taking mega-doses of laughter.

If you would keep at it long enough, I am sure that laughter would be as sound an aerobic exercise as jogging, and it's much easier on the knees, unless, of course, you are a knee slapper in the process.

Now, you tell me. When do you feel better than when you are laughing?

> **It is NORMAL for parenthood to be filled with surprises—and joys.**

Laughter is also good medicine for the parent-child relationship. And it is one of those medicines where you really can't overdose. The more the better.

However, to be most effective, the dosage must be about the same for everybody involved. If one person is laughing and another one isn't, then probably somebody is laughing at somebody else. And that isn't healthy—that's cruel.

Your Family's Laughter Potential

Laughter, like many other medicines, can be manufactured out of artificial materials. If you sense that your relationship needs a healthy dose of laughter, you could buy a joke book, rent old Abbott and Costello movies, or stay up past midnight when everybody gets giddy and giggles for no apparent reason.

> *If I had known my child would become such a pleasant adult, I would have grown up much earlier than I did.*

Although I say this partly in fun, I do intend it as something of a practical suggestion. There are those times when the family just really needs to laugh. Something has happened. There has been too much tension. Nerves are raw. The world is on edge. In other words, everybody needs a good laugh. When those times come, you may want to prime the pump a bit.

Of course, the risk in this is a matter of taste. Some members of the family may not find the chosen artificial materials as funny as some other member of the family does. When that time comes, there is a need for something called compromise, and compromise itself rarely produces much laughter.

But there is another source of laughter in families. There is always a great opportunity for organic laughter—or laughter that grows out of normal situations when normal people do normal things.

This kind of laughter is a matter of location. It's the result of standing on the right side of an issue or event. Most family issues or events have two sides. One side could be tense or maybe even ugly at times. The other side is the one that provokes all the people involved to laughter. To determine whether this is an issue which has a laughter-potential side, you can apply the ten-year test. Just think ahead ten years. If this is going to be funny ten years from now, then it has inherent laughter potential now. If you find yourself standing on the tense and ugly side, you may want to run around to the other side where all the laughter is.

I know about this organic laughter in families by more than personal experience. I have done extensive research. At least one million people have told me that someday they are going to write a really funny book about the hilarious family events they have collected through the years.

Natural Comedians

Obviously those people probably won't all get a book written. If they did, there wouldn't be anybody left to read the books. But it is refreshing to see so many people who find so much medicine in their own families.

And why not? Years ago I observed that children are all natural comedians. Who else would have enough sense of humor to enjoy what they enjoy? You pick it up. They throw it down again. What a fun game, except for the adult who has to play it, too. You cover your face and they giggle. I have tried to understand that one logically, but I don't think humor withstands the test of logic.

> I tell you the truth, anyone who will not receive the kingdom of God like a little child will never enter it.
> *Mark 10:15*

If you are a normal parent with normal children, you surely will have had at least one opportunity to experience the sheer hilarity of having a child don his mother's underwear as a hat while parading proudly throughout the neighborhood.

That's one of those sight jokes where you have to be there. It's funnier to see than tell about.

But it is a standard game during growing season, and children are the only comedians with the natural ability to pull it off.

> It is NORMAL for grandparents to be less objective as grandparents than they were as parents.

In more recent years, I have observed that adolescents are natural comedians, too. I discovered that on those occasions when I volunteered to direct high-school plays. Regardless of their age, these students always yell, "Let's do a comedy. We're all so funny anyway." Frequently, that little outburst would come from people who hadn't even grinned for six weeks. But they still saw themselves as humorists.

Now that I have grown well into middle age, I have also begun to observe that adults are natural comedians, too. Therefore, since we already have all these comedians in the family, we may as well have some laughter. That should be the normal consequence.

Vulnerability

Of course, organic laughter does require one natural fertilizer—vulnerability. If we are going to get any laughter out of normal family situations, somebody is going to have to be bold enough to hold his escapades up for scrutiny and possible laughter.

A few years ago I walked a mile and a half home from work one evening and left the car in the parking lot. Now, I didn't particularly enjoy walking back down in the cold night to retrieve my automobile. But my family enjoyed it. They enjoyed it that night, and they have enjoyed it often since. Once I overcame the initial shock of being vulnerable, I decided to enjoy it, too. Now, I actually feel a little noble about having contributed to the laughter collection of our family.

But these kinds of things happen in normal families and happen often. We may as well stand on the laughter side because it's healthier for us personally and for the family than making an event or an issue more serious than it needs to be.

I have a friend who is presently undergoing one of those really tough stages of an individual's life. His daughter just turned thirteen years old. We can talk about the stress of transitions—marriage, graduation, changing jobs, moving, retirement—but one of the most stressful transitions for many people is to become parents of an adolescent.

In this transition at least two people—parent and child—suffer stress so that the level doesn't just double; it grows exponentially.

Children are a great comfort in your old age—and they help you to reach it faster, too.

LIONEL KAUFMAN

My friend was suffering normal stress. He and his daughter were having difficulty communicating. She was crying a lot. Her grades were sagging. She was busy dropping old friends and picking up new ones that he didn't know. In short, there wasn't much joy in the relationship.

One day he read in some publication like *Parents Magazine* that the thing he should do is to develop some mutual activity with his daughter. Since she was already a talented gymnast, he decided that that should be the appropriate activity for the two of them to share and build the relationship.

After a few days' practice, he entered them both in a father-daughter tumbling meet. The daughter performed well, but father performed a little less than well. After doing everything poorly, he came to the floor exercise. He promptly did his back flip, landed on his shoulder off the mat, and had to be carried out on a stretcher.

That night, after the rest of the family had retired, the father went in to see the daughter. In the dark of her room, that thirteen-year-old girl told her dad that when he was out there performing so poorly, she was in the stands more embarrassed than she had ever been in her life.

But after she had had time to think about it, she told herself that anyone who would go to those lengths to make a fool out of himself just to be near his daughter must love her a lot.

At that point, the two of them started laughing, and there is still laughter in the relationship. Maybe someday, one of them will write a book.

ASSURANCE
CHECK

It is normal for people not to enjoy taking tests because they are usually such painful ordeals. But this little check sheet is designed to be just the opposite. It is designed to bring a little assurance into this office of parenthood.

Go down through the list and check each item for which you can say, "I know how that feels."

When you have finished, you will probably have enough checks to warrant your saying, "Maybe my children aren't so bad after all."

And that should provide a little balm.

___ 1. It is normal for a baby to be late. We can predict tornadoes, hurricanes, and the outcomes of political campaigns, but babies still come when they get ready.

___ 2. It is normal for a small baby to cry at night and sleep during the day. Come to think of it, that's normal for a fifteen-year-old, too.

___ 3. It is normal for a two-year-old not to be cute on command. Be forewarned. When you brag about your child, use words you won't mind eating, should the need arise later.

___ 4. It is normal for potty training to come with a certain number of setbacks.

___ 5. It is normal for grandparents to be less objective as grandparents than they were as parents.

___ 6. It is normal for a child to cry a bit the first day of school. It is particularly normal for moms to cry the first day of school.

___ 7. It is normal for junior-high students to look at the shopping mall as a Temple of Mating Rituals.

___ 8. It is normal for a nine-year-old not to enjoy sitting in plastic school chairs for six-hour blocks of time. Normal reactions to these conditions might include squirming, shuffling, squealing, punching, poking, and provoking, any of which might be severe enough to draw reprimands from the adults in charge who may or may not have to sit in plastic chairs.

___ 9. It is normal for ninth-graders to be tardy for class. It is also normal that one or all of the following excuses could be accurate.

My locker stuck.

I had to go to the bathroom.

The teacher kept me after class.

I saw my counselor in the hall.

My friend was crying.

I fell down the stairs.

I dropped my pencil.

I got yelled at for running in the hall.

It's too far to come.

___10. It's normal for a child to have a higher appreciation of food art than the adults at the table do.

___11. It's normal for seniors to goof off the last quarter. That doesn't just apply to high-school seniors; it's even worse in college seniors.

___12. It is normal for that early adolescent whose foot size matches his age to spill something at every meal, to stumble just walking across a clean carpet, and to bump his head on the door on the way to his own room. It is also normal for that same marvel to skateboard down the sidewalk at forty miles per hour while eating a snowcone, while reading *Sports Illustrated*, and listening to New Kids on the Block on his boombox.

___13. It is normal for children to think their parents are infallible so they say such things as, "My daddy is stronger than your daddy." It also is normal for adolescents to think their parents are totally and completely incompetent so they say such things as, "That is sooooo dumb."

___14. It is normal for teachers to look stern during normal parent teacher conferences. If you were walking through the woods and suddenly had to confront a bear face to face, how would you look?

___15. It is normal for thirteen-year-olds to stand on their toes and say to their shortest parent, "Look, I'm as tall as you are."

___16. It is normal for people who are not parents to watch normal parents, and make a list of those things they will never do when they become parents. It is also normal for those people to throw that list away about six weeks after the first child is born.

___17. It is normal for a sixteen-year-old to show absolutely no interest in the parent's profession. It is also normal for that same child to enter the parent's profession ten years later.

___18. It is normal for children to enjoy the box more than the toy. *Moral: Give empty boxes for Christmas.*

___19. It is normal for children of all ages to leave doors open. That includes refrigerator doors, car doors, and outside doors.

___20. It is normal for that adolescent who wouldn't even boil water at home to be an excellent employee when he works for the people down the street.

___21. It is normal for an early adolescent to resist any attempts to hug him and cry three days later because you don't ever hug him anymore.

___22. It is normal for some children to enjoy hammering more than they enjoy reading.

___23. It is normal for a child to walk through a puddle, even if he has to go out of his way to find it.

___24. It is normal for any child of any age to think that she is not bright enough, not pretty enough, not talented enough, or not popular enough.

___25. It is normal for adolescents to have vocabularies that include: "Soooo," "You don't trust me," "I'm so humilified," "Nobody likes me," "I want to move away from home."

___26. It is normal for parents to suffer pangs of guilt.

___27. It is normal for parenthood to be filled with surprises—and joys.